GROWING UP YINZER

···

MEMORIES FROM BELOVED PITTSBURGHERS

DICK ROBERTS

FOREWORD BY BETSY BENSON

THE
History
PRESS

Published by The History Press
Charleston, SC
www.historypress.com

Cover images: Front: Donnie Iris. First row: Patrice King Brown, George Benson, Jeff Goldblum and Swin Cash. Second row: Bill Cowher, Mark Cuban, Lynne Hayes-Freeland, Rick Sebak and Billy Porter. Back: Joe Namath, Tony Dorsett and Dan Marino.

Cover design and illustration by Rob Rogers.

First published 2023

Manufactured in the United States

ISBN 9781467152044

Library of Congress Control Number: 2023938577

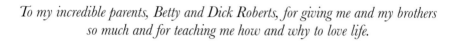

To my incredible parents, Betty and Dick Roberts, for giving me and my brothers so much and for teaching me how and why to love life.

To my wife, Karen, for her extraordinary mind and her open heart.

And to my beautiful and kind twin daughters, Delaney and Deirdre, may they always find happiness wherever they are.

CONTENTS

Foreword, by Betsy Benson   7
Acknowledgements   9
Introduction   11

BUSINESS
Bill Strickland   13
John Dick   16
Joe Pytka   20
Mark Cuban   23
Ray Werner   25
Rich Engler   28

POLITICS
Michael Hayden   32
Tom Murphy   35
David Morehouse   39

SPORTS
Bill Cowher   43
Dick Groat   46
Jim Kelly   49
John Calipari   51
Suzie McConnell-Serio   54
Swin Cash   57
Tony Dorsett   60
Dan Marino   62
Joe Namath   64
Sonny Vaccaro   67

CONTENTS

ENTERTAINMENT

Ahmad Jamal	71
Antoine Fuqua	73
Billy Gardell	76
Billy Hartung	78
Billy Porter	80
Burton Morris	82
Chris Frantz	85
Donnie Iris	89
Ed Driscoll	92
George Benson	95
Jeff Goldblum	97
Joe Negri	100
Joe Saylor	103
Ken Gargaro	105
Maria Caruso	108
Michael Campayno	110
Rob Marshall	113
Frank Nicotero	115
Roger Humphries	118
Tom Savini	121

EDUCATION

Ken Gormley	124
Samuel Hazo	128
Evan Wolfson	130

BROADCAST

Amanda Balionis Renner	134
Bob Pompeani	136
Ellis Cannon	139
Jim Krenn	141
Joy Taylor	144
Larry Richert	146
Lynne Hayes-Freeland	149
Rick Sebak	151
Patrice King Brown	154

Sources	157
About the Author	159

FOREWORD

Pittsburgh tends to pass its unique characteristics on to its residents like genetic traits. Or is it the other way around? Have the children of Pittsburgh created their hometown's character over time? Maybe it's a little bit of both. Yes, I think Pittsburghers are born and made. They're a product of unique upbringings that can inform and delight—if you are lucky enough to get one in a talkative mood.

As it turns out, Dick Roberts is quite talented at getting his carefully selected "Yinzers" not just to talk but to open up and share poignant details about their upbringings, details that go quite a way in understanding what makes Pittsburgh such a distinctive place. He has thoughtfully picked Pittsburghers from a spectrum of backgrounds and experiences and coaxed them to share what their parents taught them, to remember who inspired them, to recount tales from the past.

As a whole, this collection of stories fills a gap in the lexicon of local lore, and most importantly, it's a joy to read. As you would expect, certain themes emerge. Yes, many of these Yinzers come from modest means and tightly knit families. And thankfully, they remain modest and genuine in their accounts. We Pittsburghers have a certain pride of ownership in our most successful natives, and this collection proves those feelings were well placed.

The character of our town—and the characters who reside or were raised within it—is the sum total of its rugged terrain, role as a confluence for war and commerce, skill at making things, quirky Appalachian accent, slice-and-dice neighborhoods, tightly knit families, ethnic roots and the list goes on.

—Betsy Benson

ACKNOWLEDGEMENTS

There is an African proverb that it takes a village to raise a child, but it also takes a village to write a book. Nothing could be closer to the truth in this case.

Over the years, I've heard Pittsburghers talk about growing up here and what it has meant to them. So when I thought that a collection of such stories would make for an interesting book, I really had no idea of how to go about doing that. What I did know was that I didn't want to make rookie mistakes, and I would need to listen to the experts to help guide me.

Strangely enough, I also thought about Bill Cowher and his retirement press conference when he made it clear that he was leaving Pittsburgh and proclaimed, "I'm one of you. *Yinz* know what I mean?" With the general idea for the book in my head and Coach Cowher's use of a word that's meant to foster camaraderie with Pittsburghers in mind, *Growing Up Yinzer* was born.

Wondering if I was on the right track, I initially conducted an investigation and a created foolproof method to ensure acceptance of the concept: I hit up my family, colleagues and friends from college, including Joe Carlucci, Woody DeBlasio and Howard Algeo. With their affirmation, I created a synopsis and submitted it, with the help of Giant Eagle's Wendy Stover, to Arcadia Publishing and The History Press in Mount Pleasant, South Carolina, for review.

I didn't know what I was getting myself into. Working on this book over a period of eighteen months—in between working full time with clients and managing our Pittsburgh Yinzer Greetings business—has been informative, invigorating and gratifying. Its completion was made possible only through the support, encouragement, affability and diligence of family, friends, publishing professionals and collaborators.

The greatest blessing to me has been my wife, Karen, and the presence of our twin daughters, Delaney and Deirdre, in my life. They have been there all the way. I would have never engaged in this endeavor had it not been for their unending inspiration, insights, wisdom, technical support and cheerful optimism.

I am appreciative of Betsy Benson, publisher of *Pittsburgh Magazine* and a friend and colleague for twenty-five years, for being an enthusiastic advocate. I was delighted and honored for her contributing the foreword that added immeasurably to the work.

My friend Lloyd Stamy, the author of *Reunion of Strangers, Strangers No More* and, most recently, *Perfect Stranger: Bad Bear Down*, provided superb advice and sound judgment.

At Arcadia Publishing, I am especially grateful to Chief Executive Officer Brittain Phillips for supporting this project. Acquisitions Editor Banks Smither understood this book from the beginning and has been a wise counselor every step of the way. A special thanks to Banks for rolling up his sleeves, bringing great care to our collaborative effort, guiding it along and getting us to the finish line.

I owe special thanks to all of the storytellers, without whom these personal, first-person narratives would not have been possible. I hope that each of you knows how much I value the time you spent with me and how much I admire your undying love for your hometown. I am especially indebted to the early adopters who were so willing to participate from the outset: Chris Frantz, Frank Nicotero, Tom Murphy, Ken Gormley, Mark Cuban, Billy Hartung, Sonny Vaccaro and Bill Cowher.

A group of lifelong friends helped to facilitate the many contacts and interviews, and my thanks go to Tom Rooney, Marty Ashby, Lloyd Stamy, Sam Costanzo, Mary Ann Bohrer, Deb Moore, Tom McMillan, Burt Lauten, Larry Richert, Jim Krenn, Ray Werner, Sheila Hyland, E.J. Borghetti, Mark Bluestein, Brady Smith, David Sedelmeier, Frank Murgia, Harry Hayden, Chris Cotugno and Audrey Glickman.

Finally, there is an idiom to "not judge the book by its cover." In this case, you can, as Rob Rogers brought his great talent to bring the book cover to life with his colorful, illustrative style, and I am grateful for him marching along with me on this wonderful journey.

INTRODUCTION

There was not a Roberts on that boat, but I grew up in an Italian family who, not unusually, put great import on food and storytelling. My parents owned the Darlington Inn, a tavern and restaurant in Ligonier, Pennsylvania, that featured Italian food, and their cooking was exceptional.

There was a daily, almost obsessive focus on the quality of the ingredients, the cultural traditions and the stories around the dinner table about past and present events that helped make sense of our life experiences. It ended up heightening my interest in all things narrative.

Perhaps the thing that makes us human is the stories that each of us has. Many people think that the gift of storytelling belongs only to writers, shamans and the very old. The reality is that we are all storytellers from the very earliest days of our lives.

We are our stories. Stories told within a family or in a culture become even more powerful as they are shared year after year. They become part of who we are, what we believe and how we see our future.

As a decades-long communications practitioner, my love of storytelling and all that it encompasses only continues to grow every year. It has been one of the most valuable resources in my toolbox. Storytelling can raise awareness of history and community and help us understand others and ourselves. In those stories, we often feel empathy with the characters we encounter.

While I grew up a little more than an hour from Pittsburgh, I always felt connected to the city. By reading the *Pittsburgh Press* or watching KDKA TV every day, it didn't take me long to realize that "Yinzer" and "Jagoff" are terms of endearment and that saying "dahtahn" is as much a beloved tradition as putting fries on your sammich or waving a yellow towel.

That's why I created *Growing Up Yinzer*, to provide a vibrant, varied, thought-provoking and entertaining collection of first-person stories and memories that share the sights, sounds, joys, successes, failures and vitality of life through the eyes of fifty-one well-known Pittsburghers.

It's fair to say that most Pittsburghers would agree that growing up in Western Pennsylvania is pretty special. After all, we lay claim to one of the best children's entertainers (Mister Rogers), amusement parks (Idlewild and Kennywood Park), sports teams and players and community parks.

What more could we want? By growing up in Pittsburgh, you came to learn how to be good to your neighbor by letting an elderly person go ahead of you in the Giant Eagle checkout line. You didn't visit a therapist growing up—you dealt with your anger issues during Steeler games. Speaking of sports, you learned what loyalty meant when you hear names like Franco Harris, Mario Lemieux and Roberto Clemente. You knew true kindness from watching *Mister Rogers' Neighborhood*. Pittsburgh is family-centric, and it's all about community. Every kid growing up in Pittsburgh learns that from a very young age. Even if your close family isn't here, your friends are your family.

Pittsburgh has been home to a long list of amazing people: artists, performers, athletes, musicians, scientists, politicians, business and community leaders, educators, laborers and so many more. They are united by a common culture, their passion to pursue their dreams and their great stories.

Pittsburghers all know that being from the city is a huge part they carry with them throughout their lives. *Growing Up Yinzer* will enable you to meet and learn more about a collection of intriguing people and their stories, how the city has taught us all many life lessons and the many ways that growing up in Pittsburgh has shaped our very character.

BUSINESS

BILL STRICKLAND

For decades, Bill Strickland has transformed thousands of lives, restored faith in ethical leadership and reshaped the business of social change. As president and CEO of the Manchester Bidwell Corporation—an extraordinary jobs training center and community arts program—he and his staff work with corporations, community leaders and schools to give disadvantaged kids and adults the opportunities they need to build a better future.

It's a story that is continuing. It really starts in Manchester, where I grew up at an elementary school where six foreign languages were spoken. We didn't call it cultural diversity—we called it the neighborhood.

As a high school kid in a tough, diverse, working-class neighborhood that everybody gave up on for dead was where it started for me. I was just about flunking out of school, and on a Wednesday afternoon I was walking down the corridor of Oliver High School, kind of minding my own business, and there was this art teacher, Frank Ross, who made a great big old ceramic vessel. I happened to be looking in the door of the art room, and if you've ever seen clay done, it's magic. I had never seen anything like that before in my life.

I walked in the art room, and I said, "What is that," and he said, "Ceramics and who are you." I said, "I'm Bill Strickland, I want you to teach me that." And he said, "Well, get your homeroom teacher to sign a piece of paper that

Courtesy Manchester Craftsman's Guild.

says you can come here and I'll teach it to you." And so for the remaining two years of my high school, I cut all my classes, but I had the presence of mind to give the teachers' classes that I cut the pottery that I made, and they gave me passing grades and that's how I got out of high school.

If ever in life there is a clairvoyant experience, I had one that day. I saw a radiant and hopeful image of how the world ought to be. It opened up a portal for me that suggested that there might be a whole range of possibilities and experiences that I had not explored. It was night and day—literally. I saw a line and I thought: this is dark, and this is light. And I need to go where the light is. I'd watched my neighborhood go from a healthy community to a ghetto. I needed to find a way out. But there weren't many examples of successful people in my community who could serve as role models.

Mr. Ross was a public school teacher and an iconic figure in my life whose family shared the same values that my family shared. He would say, "I don't care about the color of your skin. You want to take art? I'm your guy." In effect, he really adopted me as one of his kids. And when the school closed down, Mr. Ross opened up his house. I used to take the bus to the guy's house at 3:30 in the afternoon and stay until about seven o'clock and take the bus back to the neighborhood. He took me to jazz concerts at Crawford's Grill. So why do we have a music hall many years later at the Manchester Craftsmen's Guild? Because Mr. Ross used to bring in jazz to the classroom, and I decided, someday, I'm going build a music hall and I did.

Mr. Ross said, "You're too smart to die, and I don't want it on my conscience, so I'm leaving this school and I'm taking you with me." He drove me out to the University of Pittsburgh, where I filled out a college application and got in on probation. Well, I'm now a trustee of the university, and at my installation ceremony, I said, "I'm the guy who came from the neighborhood who got into the place on probation. Don't give up on the poor kids because you never know what's going to happen to those children in life."

My view is that if you want to involve yourself in the life of people who have been given up on, you have to look like the solution and not the problem. I built a facility in the toughest neighborhood in Pittsburgh with the highest crime rate. Manchester Craftsmen's Guild is named after my neighborhood. I was adopted by the bishop of the Episcopal Diocese during the riots, and he donated a row house, and in that row house I started Manchester Craftsmen's Guild, teaching students about clay.

The other program is called Bidwell Training Center; it is a vocational school for ex–steel workers and single parents and welfare mothers. You remember we used to make steel in Pittsburgh? Well, we don't make any steel anymore, and the people who used to make the steel are having a very tough time of it. We rebuild them and give them new life.

Many of the people I work with are coming from environments in which they are academically and intellectually challenged. And so by providing industry-specific training for those students, they develop a capability, an ability to earn a living, dramatically improve their self-esteem and improve their income so that instead of liabilities they become assets in the community. And that's the key to the puzzle.

I'm the Black kid from the '60s who got his life saved with ceramics. Well, I went out and decided to reproduce my experience with other kids in the neighborhood, the theory being if you get kids flowers and you give them food and you give them sunshine and enthusiasm, you can bring them right back to life.

I have four hundred kids from the Pittsburgh public school system that come to us every day of the week for arts education. And these are children who are flunking out of public school. Last year, we put 88 percent of those kids in college, and we've averaged over 80 percent for fifteen years. We've made a fascinating discovery: there's nothing wrong with the kids that affection and sunshine and food and enthusiasm and music can't cure. For that I won a big old plaque—Man of the Year in Education. I beat out all the PhDs because I figured that if you treat children like human beings, it increases the likelihood they're going to behave that way.

Pittsburgh corporate leaders allowed me to gain a foothold and support my ideas in a way that I can't think of another community would embrace me the way this place has. That's directly because of the way I was raised. I came to view the world in color, not black and white. That's why you see the center looking the way it looks. Now in an industrial park, the school houses a series of programs, including youth arts, vocational training, horticulture, agriculture and technology. We believe that our history of programs that started under impossible economic and social circumstances and were transformed into world-class arts and education organizations continues to serve as a powerful source of hope locally and internationally.

It shaped my view of how I could contribute to making the world a better place. I felt a responsibility to take the lessons that I learned to make them real. The thing about Pittsburgh is the people are very real. They've had lives that had challenges, immigrants, Black folks—and they figured out how to move past that and make themselves part of the general community. That's why I'm doing this work.

Art is a way of thinking about life. It's a language, and we've been able to so far master the language of speaking the arts in real time, not in a museum sense, but in a life sense. Dizzy Gillespie came here, and I took him around for a tour. He said, "You're a hell of a jazz musician." I said I don't play music, and he said, "Yes you do. This school is your song." So the kids are living the art. They're eating the art in the culinary program, they are practicing the arts. Every day it becomes their vocabulary.

Every day I run into students now who have their own families and whose kids are going to college and people who have graduated from companies like Bayer and Calgon Carbon. You see hard evidence of the return on the investment, so it's not theoretical. This is actually real and measured in real time, and that's a very gratifying way to make a living.

JOHN DICK

John Dick is a serial entrepreneur with an improbable career that started with Fred Rogers helping him choose a college; that segued into a stint as an aide to Senator Rick Santorum, then swerved to co-founding lobbying firm GSP Consulting and, in 2008, starting CivicScience Inc. He is the host of the successful podcast The Dumbest Guy in the Room *and author of* What We're Seeing, *the weekly e-mail newsletter read by a who's-who of business leaders, policymakers and celebrities. Dick is also a frequent speaker at the Carnegie Mellon University Swartz Center for Entrepreneurship, a contributing writer for* AdAge, Microsoft News *and* Forbes *and has appeared on* Good Morning

America *and* Yahoo! Finance *and as a regular guest on* Cuomo *on* NewsNation. *He is the lead singer of Moscow Mule, an alternative rock cover band, and a recipient of the distinguished Jefferson Award for his charitable works.*

I grew up in Westmoreland County, about thirty miles east of the city, and my mom's family was from the Bedford area so I kind of split time between the two. But I always considered myself being from Pittsburgh. We were pretty much middle-class kids, great family, super close with my dad. My dad was by far the biggest influence in my life, my best friend, the best man at my wedding.

My dad worked at Pittsburgh National Bank, a PNC predecessor, suit and tie, cufflinks every day, but we spent the rest of our lives pretty much around rural to certainly blue-collar neighbors. I watched my dad, not in a disingenuous way, adapt to both situations. From the time that we were little, my parents had two Christmas parties at our house every year. The Friday party was for all of his work friends from Mount Lebanon, the north hills and other areas who would drive the whole way out to North Huntingdon. The Saturday party were friends from his childhood, from places like Jeannette Manor, so it was two different vibes. I asked my dad why two parties instead of just one, and he said that he felt everybody would feel better if it was a bit more familiar.

One of the things that is interesting about Pittsburgh compared to a lot of other larger cities is that a forty-minute commute can take you really far from the city's urban core and be in the country. You can live in a place like that and work in a metropolitan area, whereas a forty-minute commute in New York takes you three square miles from Manhattan. It gave us the

Courtesy Civic Science.

opportunity to have that well-rounded experience and enabled this unique degree of familiarity and even solidarity for people across socioeconomic and cultural lines. I picked up on that and learned how to be more empathetic to the situation other people are in and how to make other people feel more comfortable. That's such an important feature of our region, particularly in today's politically divisive world.

The late Fred Rogers had a big impact on my life. He was a close family friend. My father was in the charitable endowments department at PNB, and one of the clients was the Fred Rogers' Foundation. We'd see him and Joanne a few times a year, and I went to Rollins College because of Fred Rogers. He asked my father, "Where's J.T. thinking of going to school?" My dad said, "He's figuring it out." Fred said, "Has he looked at Rollins?" which was Fred's alma mater. Next thing you know, Fred mailed me a VHS tape about the school. I still have the envelope. He and Joanne had a house near the school and went there every January. I'd go over to have lunch with them and sometimes take a friend. It was a very coveted invitation. And they served peanut butter and jelly sandwiches and chocolate milk. True story.

At Rollins, I was a bit homesick initially, but I started to meet people from all over the country and started to think maybe I won't go back to Pittsburgh. I was going to go to law school, and my advisor at school suggested that I get a job with a politician or a judge to bolster my résumé. Coincidentally, I got a job working for first-term Senator Rick Santorum, who I knew nothing about, but it was a job with a U.S. senator.

I didn't intend to be an entrepreneur, definitely not. I stumbled upon a business idea I couldn't shake. I was working in politics with the thought of going to law school. The idea of GSP rattled into my brain, and I couldn't ignore it. In retrospect, there's nothing I'd rather be. I just didn't know that when I was twenty-two.

I was twenty-four when we started GSP, and it was pretty successful pretty fast. The quality of the idea was strong enough to overcome my inadequacies as a businessperson at that time. I never appreciated that until much later. When your business is going well, it tends to be a function of luck, things beyond your control and the value of having a great business partner.

At CivicScience, we combine some really kick-ass software that was built by folks at Carnegie Mellon with a really large database, and we capture survey data. Really clever model. We've embedded polls inside of hundreds of different web properties that allow us to engage people while they're reading content. It allows us to gather consumer data at a really unprecedented scale. People answer nearly 7 million of our poll questions every day.

We have a team in Pittsburgh that writes questions every day based on what's going on in the news so we can report to our clients within a few hours of news breaking about something or a product recall or what have you, a bad PR event for someone, what the U.S. take is on that situation. Once we validated that the data was accurate and actionable and, more importantly, predictive of other things, we started to build a very healthy business around that.

It allows us to study everything, and our ethos is that everything affects everything, and everything is constantly changing. So we study everything constantly. That's the general idea. We're adding, we're tracking a couple of hundred thousand survey questions at any time and studying the marriage between all of those things.

We are proud to be in Pittsburgh and to be part of Pittsburgh and the tech community here. Pittsburgh is an amazing place to build a company. Even in 2007 and 2008, Pittsburgh still had a bit of its smoky image. I can remember very vividly when I would fly to California or New York to meet with investors, they would say, "Where are you from?" I would say Pittsburgh, and I would get this sort of sneer but I would tell them that the technical talent coming from CMU is second to none. I watched that reaction go from "Oh, Pittsburgh" to "Ohhhh, Pittsburgh!" I'm telling everyone we're here, that's why we're here, our entire team was plucked out of that school, our intellectual property was plucked out of that school and that became a huge contributor to our success. Now it's the first thing on our website: we're from Pittsburgh. The first slide of my investor deck says Pittsburgh-based.

We have affordable office space in a vibrant and fun part of the city, where half of our team can walk to work. My favorite aspect of Pittsburgh is the growing network of other start-ups and entrepreneurs here who go out of their way to help each other. There are a lot of people here who not only want to build special companies but really care about being part of Pittsburgh's renaissance. We're always referring each other new business, sharing resources and just getting together to learn from each other.

I can say confidently, whatever modest success I've had to date, I wouldn't have had a fraction of it without Pittsburgh. A lot of it is the serendipity of the people and things that just happen to be here and then the people who have gone out of their way to support us, to support me, because of those Pittsburgh connections. As a result, you won't find many people who are bigger patriots about Pittsburgh than I am.

JOE PYTKA

Filmmaker Joe Pytka is creator of some of the best and most well-known television commercials ever made. Pytka has directed more than five thousand ads for some of the world's largest corporations and earned many awards and nominations, including three Directors Guild of America Commercial Direction Awards and fifteen nominations. For more than four decades, his stylized images have become part of the American consciousness, and his commercials for clients such as Budweiser, Pepsi, McDonald's and the NFL have aired more than thirty times during the Super Bowl telecast. Those include Madonna's infamous Pepsi commercial, "Make a Wish"; a frying egg demonstrating "This is your brain on drugs"; Ray Charles's "Uh-huh" for Pepsi; and Bo Jackson's "Bo Knows" for Nike; among many others. His legendary "Hare Jordan" Super Bowl commercial for Nike featuring Michael Jordan and Bugs Bunny led directly to the animated Space Jam *feature film.*

I grew up Catholic in Braddock, a steel mill–rife suburb of Pittsburgh on the Monongahela River. Or as I told George Harrison of the Beatles when I was directing their *Free as a Bird* music video, "I'm from the Liverpool of America, Pittsburgh." That's how I got the name Joe Pittsburgh.

I was an aspiring painter and athlete. Carnegie Institute has a progressive art program that touched the Pittsburgh community in important ways. For me, the program started in the fourth grade. It took two students from each school in the community, and each year there was a winnowing-out process so that at the end of six years, there were six people that were sent to Carnegie Tech, now Carnegie Mellon, for advanced classes in painting, design and sculpture. The most accomplished student was Andy Warhol.

I was privileged to make it through the program entirely, but I owe that to Joseph Fitzpatrick. He ran the program after being one of its teachers. He was a tall, impossibly elegant gentleman who would walk past the lines of students waiting for class, greeting them, some by name, and admonishing them gently, about posture, attitude, chewing gum. Ironically, he would address me as Mister Pytka, as did Fred Rogers a few years later.

The better students were asked to be assistants to the staff, handing out pencils, crayons, paper to the students before class. For some reason, the staff disliked me, sometimes accusing me of silly transgressions. One confronted me, saying I was doing cartwheels while doling out supplies. I couldn't even do a cartwheel, but she denied my denial.

We students were called Tam O'Shanters, named after an Irish hat, but we didn't have to wear them. I thought the name was too cute, but after each class, the top six assignments were selected for that week's prize.

Courtesy Getty.

Each of these students was to go to the stage and reproduce the work on a large easel as an "inspiration" to the other students. It was called "being up on the easel." During the class, these students would introduce themselves, their name, age and school. No one was "up on the easel" more than me. My mother actually became embarrassed. Go figure.

At the end of the sixth year, it was time to inform the final six students that were to go to Carnegie Tech. I wasn't feeling very good about things. The past summer, I was passed over for a student project for the museum for who I considered lesser talents. I felt insulted because one of the student selected was a classic ass-kisser.

This particular Saturday morning, I was waiting in line for class supplies and Mr. Fitzpatrick stopped, greeted me and asked if I had been notified of Carnegie Tech.

"No, sir."

"You haven't?"

"No, sir."

He looked at me for a while, then turned and walked away. He came back a few minutes later. "There was a misunderstanding. You'll be going to Tech in the fall."

I don't remember anything about my thanking him or any circumstances being explained. He obviously went to bat for me. Mr. Fitzpatrick was the most elegant, genteel man I have ever met. His most famous student was Andy Warhol. I regret I was never able to thank him properly for allowing me this privilege.

Then, on my father's wish—keep in mind he was a foreman at Westinghouse—I began studying chemical engineering at the University of Pittsburgh because he suggested it was a way to make a practical living. I loathed it beyond imagination, but it gave me an opportunity to play basketball at the collegiate level for one year with Don Hennon, who was a great player. I decided to drop out of Pitt and began my filmmaking career at WRS Motion Picture and Video Lab, working on new technology and equipment with George Romero, who was then a fledgling filmmaker.

At WRS, I became well versed in editing, shooting and recording techniques. I formed a relationship and started shooting and editing shows for WQED and working on documentaries in various capacities like *Steeltown Blues* about my hometown of Braddock; *Maggie's Farm*; and a documentary on air pollution narrated by Orson Welles. The thing that was great about Pittsburgh was it was the third-largest corporate headquarters city in the country at that time, so there was a lot of money to support the arts and we were able to do a lot of things at QED as a result.

I shot a forerunner to music videos called *High Flying Bird*, featuring Steve McQueen in a four-wheel-drive truck traveling Mexican landscapes. I really began shooting commercials in between the documentaries, including some Iron City Beer spots in actual taverns, including one that re-created a Polish wedding.

It was my background in painting that drew me to the formality of commercials, and my approach to commercial making was a major turning point in my life. I had done these documentaries that were fairly emotional, and I wanted to get to that point in my commercial work, working with real people in real situations. At the time, no one was doing it. Commercials were real theatrical. As good as Howard Zieff's commercials were and are, they were very theatrical. For about two or three years in Pittsburgh, I was doing these commercials for Iron City where we would go somewhere with real people. Those commercials were very successful because commercials are supposed to entertain you—they were entertainments, make people feel good.

It's important not to lose sight of the overall goal, which is to capture those "real" moments and performances. That's what I try for in commercials. I'm not comfortable as any sort of labeled director. I'm not necessarily a commercial director, even though I made a lot of commercials. I'm not an actor's director, even though I like actors. I'm a filmmaker. If anything, the definitions between the kinds of directors aren't as profound as they once were; I've done a little bit of everything.

Pittsburgh was most important for, and I hate this term, my creative development. Going to art school every Saturday for much of my life, from third grade to senior year in high school, then two days a week during the summer was an incredible experience.

WQED was a flagship station for Public Broadcasting, better than New York. We did all of this incredible work that was supported by the local business community, that we could never have done anywhere else—the documentaries plus the dramatic programming. And fortunately, Ketchum, McLeod & Grove was Wieden and Kennedy before there was Wieden and Kennedy; they had good clients and did all of this terrific work that we would collaborate on.

I would shoot in California and I couldn't wait to get back to Pittsburgh. I would shoot in New York and I couldn't wait to get back to Pittsburgh. I lived there and I loved the city, and if I didn't have the opportunities that I did in other places, I would have stayed there. People in Pittsburgh, because of the hard work, care for each other. If you were driving down the street and someone in front of you had a flat tire, you would pull over and help them. Find that out here in Los Angeles—it doesn't happen anywhere else. People care for each other there because of the hard work of the steel mills and other things.

MARK CUBAN

Mark Cuban is an American billionaire entrepreneur, television personality and media proprietor. He displayed a penchant for business from a very young age and wasted no time in rising to the top echelons of the business world. Today, Cuban is the owner of the NBA club Dallas Mavericks, Landmark Theaters, Magnolia film production house and AXS HDTV network. He is the primary investor in the ABC reality TV series Shark Tank *and has authored a book titled* How to Win in the Sport of Business.

I grew up in a working-class family, just a normal kid, nothing unique or special about it at all. Up until seventh grade, I was one of only two Jewish kids at school and in the neighborhood. Then I moved a few blocks to a new school, and that changed who my schoolmates were.

It was great growing up on Bower Hill Road. I was close to all of my friends, we had access to fields to play ball on, you name it. I loved growing up in Lebo. With my brothers Brian and Jeff, we quickly found comfort in our new community. I attended Jefferson Junior High School, and sports played an important part of my new life.

As far as shaping me as an adult, I think the education I got at Mount Lebanon was critical. I think that Mount Lebanon, my family and my friends all taught me that anything was possible. I made some of my best lifetime friends at Mount Lebanon—they are still some of my best friends, and we stay in close contact. I get back to Pittsburgh at least once a year, and we take in a game.

I feel that I had great relationships with my teachers, and while I don't want to point out specifically who inspired me—there are just too many—if any of them are still teaching then they are my favorites.

Family for sure was my greatest influence. Neither of my parents had gone to college, but they pushed me to get an education to do things they were never able to do. All of my grandparents came to the United States around the age of twenty. My mom's mom was from Lithuania. Her dad was from Bessarabia. On my dad's side, my grandparents were from the south of Ukraine, and they had the typical experience: no English, no

Courtesy Texas Business Hall of Fame.

money, stay with family, find any job you could, experience the Depression and more.

That certainly shaped my parents' upbringing and, in turn, shaped mine. And as far as their name, they really didn't change their name—people just started writing it as Cubin or Cuban. As it turns out, on my dad's birth certificate, his name is spelled Cubin, and on mine it's Cuban. No one knows why!

Pittsburgh was a blue-collar town where the best summer job a kid could get was working in the mills. We always had the attitude that we could get a job, work hard and value family. That definitely helped me create a mindset of self-reliance and helped prepare me to be a better entrepreneur.

People thought I might go to work at a mill. My mom wanted me to learn how to lay carpet because she was concerned about my future. Nobody had high hopes for me, but I was a hustler. I started by buying and selling baseball cards in the local park when I was nine or ten years old. I was selling trash bags door to door. I have always been selling, always something going on. That was my nature. I just have always had an entrepreneurial bent for as long as I can remember. I was in Junior Achievement and would take the bus from my house every week, downtown, to go learn how to start and run a company. It was an incredible experience.

I was so motivated to be a successful businessperson that when my high school didn't allow me into a senior-level economics class as a junior, I started taking classes at night at Pitt. That gave me the confidence to drop out my senior year and take classes at Pitt. And because Pitt didn't have a business school then, I transferred to Indiana University in Bloomington, which allowed me to get the business education that helped me get to where I am today.

It shows everyone that the American Dream is alive and well. If the entrepreneurs on *Shark Tank* can be successful, so can anyone who works hard.

I would describe myself as a tech geek and got a job as a computer software salesman. But I had quit or been fired from three straight jobs, so I figured it was time to start my own company. I love entrepreneurship because that's what makes this country grow, and if I can help companies grow, I am creating jobs, I am setting foundations for future generations.

I learned early with my Pittsburgh upbringing that investing in myself has always paid off best. I tell people to be curious, be agile, be the best salesperson in the company. My Pittsburgh background has also affected how I've raised my family and manage employees. It used to be that my business was my primary focus. Now it's my kids and family that come first all the time. That sounds like Mount Lebanon through and through. If nothing else, it has made us enormous sports fans and really showed the value of closeness and hard work.

RAY WERNER

Ray Werner is a playwright, an award-winning advertising man and a bit of a musician—not to mention a bread baker. If you ask Ray directly, he'll tell you he is husband, a father and a grandfather first and foremost. He is a soft-spoken gentleman who expresses his gratitude for life's opportunities and his deep admiration for his artistic collaborators whenever he gets a chance. He is a lover of theater, of the storytelling process and of the creative community in Pittsburgh.

I come from a remarkable family with parents who taught us that life is nothing but love and relationships. Chuck and Pauline met and married in 1926. They started their family a year later in Freedom, Beaver County, in a house on the side of a hill. Heck, the whole town is on the side of a hill. When the market crashed in 1929, bringing with it 25 percent unemployment, they had three children and would have another three. I was born at the tail end of the long recovery, in 1938. Most remarkable is not that they survived under such turmoil, but that they never complained about it, rarely talked about it, unless asked, and, catch this, they left America in a better place for their children and grandchildren.

Born in 1900, my father left school when he was fourteen years old to work on the railroad, the PRR, as a brakeman and then worked his way up to yard master. When the Depression hit and jobs all but evaporated, there was no government bailout check. One of several jobs he did, our dad baked bread. Did he ever. Loads of it. Truckloads, you could say.

He and a friend baked bread all night, borrowed a truck and sold it during the day and made a dollar a day each. One of the many gifts he gave me was that he taught me to bake bread when I was sixteen. Today my business card reads, "Writer, baker, music maker." And our dad could write—short poems, usually, to our mother, and he would leave them

Courtesy Annie O'Neil.

around the house for her to discover. Ha! Who does that?

Here's a quickie for you. Dad worked the night turn, and we'd all be in bed when he got home at 7:00 a.m. Mom would leave his dinner in the fridge. One Friday morning he came home, there was a note on the table, "Dear Chuck, your dinner's in the fridge, Love, Pauline." He looks in the fridge and sees this lonely piece of fried fish staring at him. And this was before Saran wrap. So he turns the note over and writes this little poem: "Dear Pauline, This lonely fish that's on this plate has served its purpose fine, to help me think such holy thoughts of one I deem divine. Love, Chuck."

Then he puts the poem on the fish…and puts them both back in the fridge, I guess laughing at the look on Mom's face when she finds it.

Everybody wanted to be in their company. The characters who came and went in our kitchen, the songs, the stories, oh my goodness. We kids would sleep on the back porch in the summertime listening to them. That kitchen was where we got what we needed to create our success in life, each of us. Building relationships and learning how important stories are. That's how my advertising career took off and why I write plays. It's how my brother Larry became Pittsburgh's most esteemed PR professional, how Bernie created his brilliant manufacturing company, how Kathleen became a sought-after college prof and co-wrote English textbooks and how Patty and Rita, who never left Freedom, became two of the most beloved people in our town.

I grew up watching *Playhouse 90* and live drama on black-and-white TV in the 1950s. Just a kid, I dreamed of being another Paddy Chayefsky or Rod Serling. I wanted to be a writer, always secretly jotting down ideas. And so shy, so painfully shy. I went to a Capuchin Franciscan Seminary my first few years in high school, and that's where I fell in love with poetry. I loved to recite, and I got into the finals of a recitation contest for two years. My dad could recite a poem that would take your breath away. So that's where I got it. Another gift from my dad.

I think you're getting the idea that I'm a borrower—and indeed aren't we all? We borrow from our parents, our siblings, our neighbors, from our teachers, our friends, from everyone we meet. We start out with nothing and borrow everything we have, and soon learn, I hope, that we have to pay it back. Which is the way I hope to spend the rest of my life.

I didn't think I was college material and worked in steel mills for a few years and spent two years in the army, mostly in Alaska. So I went to Duquesne University to see if I could hack it. There are a few professors who really make a difference in your life, and I had Dr. Riley, who taught English. He gave us an assignment to write a paper, I'm not sure what it was about. So at class a few days later, the first thing he says is, "I want Ray Werner to read this paper for you." I was shaking, the paper was shaking and my voice was shaking. I sat down, yes, still shaking, and he said, in a very kind way, "The telling of it doesn't match the quality of the words." He then advised all of us that "while you're here in college, take a public speaking course and every chance you have, get in front of people and talk." I followed his advice and volunteered for the radio station, reading the news and playing music one night a week. That helped me gain some footing. And get my foot out of my mouth.

My last year at Duquesne, I wrote a half-hour script for a national radio contest and called it "Blind Man's Bluff." It was a comedy about a blind guy who has his aunt coming to visit who also pities him for being blind. To get rid of her, he pretends that he can see and pulls it off. We produced it at Duquesne's radio station WDUQ-FM, starring my friend Ray Schaeffer, and it ends up winning first prize. With that under my belt, I applied to the Yale School of Drama to study playwriting, and guess what! I got accepted. I spent almost two years under the guidance of the dean of playwriting, John Gassner. What I learned from him served me throughout my writing life, especially "Write for actors. Give them something to sink their teeth into. Use their talent." Yes, once again, borrowing from other people.

So, I collect what people tell me, what I read, what I hear. And Pittsburgh is one of the best places in the world for doing that. Over ninety ethnic neighborhoods, a working man's town, a turn-around town. Here's a few from my collection—"Nothing Happens until Someone Gets Excited." An account guy, Vince Drayne, came up with that, and it's been on my office wall for over fifty years. It works. Try it sometime.

Here's another one, from the Nobel playwright and poet Samuel Beckett, a few years before he died: "They say my best years are gone forever. But I wouldn't want them back, not with the fire that's in me now."

Another is "Write about what you know. And what you don't know, research." Good advice from Pittsburgh playwright and poet August Wilson. That's why there is often a Catholic thread in my plays. Even with its imperfections. It's who I am. And I got that from my mother. No surprise, then, that my last play was a musical called *Shantytown, The Ballad of Fr. James Cox*. Yes, a Yinzer, and one of our most heroic, pastor of Old St. Patrick's in the Strip who provided over 3 million meals for the homeless during the Great Depression.

A story puts a clamp on your head, and you just tell it the best you can. One of the primary themes of my work is forgiveness, which runs through several of my plays. It's difficult to find the handle, but when you do, look out. It's part of everyone's life, and I sure have needed it plenty of times.

I was asked recently by a young couple how Susan and I have stayed happily married now pushing fifty-seven years. Love, of course. And always in the wings, forgiveness. Also, while I'm flitting around like a skittish squirrel, Susan is a rock. She has lived her entire life not more than two miles from where she grew up, a stone's throw from Forbes Field and the Duquesne Gardens.

For a storyteller, Pittsburgh is a gold mine. It has a welcoming spirit that is unmatched. When I created our state tourism campaign "You've got a friend in Pennsylvania," it was really about the people and stories in Pittsburgh. It's who we are. Our character, our history, our ethnic neighborhoods. It's a richness we have that no any other city in America has in such abundance. If we ever lose it, we've lost our soul. Which is true if you're traveling through Pittsburgh or through life.

What a blessing to grow up Yinzer.

RICH ENGLER

Rich Engler has promoted more than six thousand concerts in the Pittsburgh area and other markets across the United States over his nearly fifty-five-year career as a concert promoter. The Pittsburgh Rock 'n Roll Hall of Fame honored Engler by naming him its first inductee in 2014.

I was born in New Kensington and grew up in Creighton, across the river. My father was a glass worker at the Pittsburgh Plate Glass Company. My mother worked for the county. It was very heavy blue-collar, and if you didn't work at PPG or the steel mill, you were going nowhere. My dad wanted me to go to PPG and said that maybe I could be a grinder, grinding wheels from Pullman Standard in Butler from train cars. I didn't know what I wanted, but I knew I didn't want that life.

I loved music growing up. I remember when I was sixteen I could drive to the top of Murray Hill in Creighton to listen to the *Porky Chedwick Show* to see what songs he was playing and obviously Clark Race and Art Pallan on KDKA Radio. I was absorbing everything in the music business, and I could not have known that I was following my nose of what I thought I really liked.

I went off to college to study art education at Carnegie Mellon, started a band and began to see a possible future for myself in music. I played the trumpet originally and was told that was the corniest instrument, so I said I played drums. Somewhere along the line, I realized that a life in music could be tough and that I would be wise to prepare myself. It's called "show business" for a reason. There's the show, and then there's the business. So I decided that I had better learn both when I told my parents I'm going to pursue the music business. My dad said, "Hey, that's not a career, that's a hobby," and I said, "Well, you might be right," but I felt like I could make it work. I say I never worked a day in my life. I've had stress, but I still have hair so it's all good.

In the early '60s, I was listening to the architects of rock-and-roll: Bo Diddley, Chuck Berry, Little Richard, Jerry Lee Lewis. These guys were my influence. Then when the Beatles came out, I said, oh, shit, I'm in the wrong direction. We need to change the look of our band, the feel and music of our band if we want to be present and right now.

In 1969, when I first met Cindy, my wife, I felt that it was time to take a risk. So I opened a business on Walnut Street in Shadyside called Go Attractions. At the start, I couldn't afford an apartment and an office, so I built a partition inside the office and lived in the back. The good news for me was that rock music was really catching fire: bigger productions, more sound, more lights and larger crowds. Every club, frat party and church outing had to have a band. And someone had to provide them. I wanted to be that person.

Sure, I was nervous about it. But I had the Novocain of youth going for me and believed that I would be able to make just about anything work. Before

Courtesy Rich Engler.

long, I was making more money than I would have been had I graduated from college. I started with nothing, so a living would have been acceptable at the time. But I knew what I didn't want. I didn't want to live across the tracks. I wanted something better. That's what I set out to achieve. You have to have the burning desire to succeed and the guts to turn your skis down on a double black diamond slope and go for it.

Three years later, when Cindy and I decided to get married, I had money in the bank. I bought a house way more expensive than I could ever have dreamed. The next thing I knew, instead of selling acts to clubs and colleges, I started promoting. Go Attractions, the booking agency, became Command Performance, the promoter, and I started buying acts from some talent agencies in New York. As a result, I learned the promoting business the right way, from the ground up. I did the advertising, the production and so on. Then I started to promote on my own in Youngstown, Johnstown and Erie and booked my band, the Grains of Sand, as the opening act for all of my shows. That band did really well from '68 through '74, until one important New York agent got wind of what I was doing and said, "I'm never going to sell you another act unless you stop playing drums and focus on being the promoter." That's when I got really serious.

One day in 1974, another local promoter named Pat DiCesare called me and said, "Rich, why should we compete? Let's sit down and make a deal." Again, I was making real money on my own, so I thought long and hard. Most people said, "Are you crazy? Do it!" Pat had the Civic Arena locked up at the time and had a great deal with the Syria Mosque. I had the Stanley Theatre deal kind of put together, which is where I was doing most of my shows. So Pat and I struck a deal. We called ourselves DiCesare-Engler Productions, and boom! Things started to happen. We set out to build the best company that we could possibly build, and within a couple of years we ranked second behind Bill Graham nationally according to *Billboard* magazine. The next thing I knew, we owned the Stanley Theatre, opened the I.C. Light Amphitheater at Station Square, opened the amphitheater at Harvey's Lake in Scranton and was operating the Tussey Mountain Amphitheater in State College. These were all groundbreaking—no one had ever done it.

In the years to come, we had all the great shows. We had Bruce Springsteen at the Syria Mosque when he was on the cover of *Newsweek* and *TIME*. We had ZZ Top's Texas Tour at Three Rivers Stadium. We had Pink Floyd. You name it. Music was still a passion for a lot of people, and wonderful things kept happening. Pittsburgh was not a "must play" market before the Stanley

Theatre. It was considered a mill town—"let's not go"—but the Stanley put Pittsburgh on the map.

In the late '90s, a huge entertainment company called SFX did a roll-up of all the regional mom-and-pop promotion companies across the United States. DiCesare-Engler was part of that roll-up. If Pat and I hadn't sold DiCesare-Engler in '98, we would have been snuffed out, no question. But the sale was a happy day for two reasons: we made some money, and we took away the inevitable pain of battling to survive. Pat went on with real estate, and I joined the troops in the bigger army, becoming the regional head for Clear Channel for a while. It was a difficult adjustment in many ways, but I know it was the right thing to do.

You know, for a while in my life, I felt a bit guilty for having more than some other people. But it's all the direct result of hard work and risk. In order to make the big bucks, you have to accept risk. You have to be able to leave your comfort zone. And that's very difficult. You have to think positive thoughts. You have to be fearless in some ways but also calculating. Even if you think you're doing the right thing and you're making money, there's probably a better way to do it. If you step up, you can make it.

As I've always told my kids, "I don't care what you do, just try to do it the best that anybody's ever done it." If you're going to be a janitor, just be the best janitor you can be, and guess what? You'll probably end up owning a janitorial business and make a million dollars. This applies to everybody. And even if you can't afford it financially, if you're doing a great job and you're smart, you will find someone who has money and will invest in you. Just go out and do it.

POLITICS

MICHAEL HAYDEN

Michael Hayden served as a U.S. Air Force four-star general and former director of the National Security Agency and principal deputy director of National Intelligence. In May 2006, General Hayden was sworn in as the director of the Central Intelligence Agency, where he served until February 2009.

In my seventy-eight years, I have been part of many different families. First, of course, was my birth family. My parents, Harry and Sadie, raised me; my sister, Debby; and my brother, Harry, on the North Side of Pittsburgh on the site of Three Rivers Stadium and now Heinz Field. The neighborhood was great, tucked between the main line of the Pennsylvania Railroad and the north bank of the Allegheny River. It could fairly be called industrial, with some light manufacturing, including Clark Candy, lots of truck parks and a good number of bars.

Like a lot of folks from that part of the country, we were a blue-collar family. Life was pretty straightforward with family, work, church, school and sports. The place was typically ethnic—Irish, Italian, one square block African American—and old-country identities were still strong. The neighborhood was largely Catholic. You could see most everybody at Sunday Mass at St. Peter's, and most of the kids—and there were a lot of them—attended the church grade school run by the Sisters of Mercy.

Sports were everyone's outlet. Throw a ball out and it would draw a crowd, no matter the season. Not that there were any proper fields. There was nothing anywhere near us that could be called a lawn. There was one small concrete playground, an unpaved parking lot or two and then there was always the street. "Go deep. Hook at the Buick, I'll hit you there." There was always enthusiasm for local sports teams or heroes. You could collect enough "pop" bottles around the neighborhood on a weekday summer morning to make enough money for streetcar fare and a $1.50 general admission ticket to sit behind Roberto Clemente in right field at Forbes Field.

And then there were the Steelers. Another St. Peter's parish family was named Rooney; they owned the football club. Oldest son Dan—later president of the team and still later ambassador to Ireland for President Barack Obama—coached the grade school football team, and I was his quarterback in the eighth grade. "The only kid who could remember the plays" was his explanation.

Mom and dad took great care of us, limited only by their resources. Supper was always a family event. Although it was the usual basic Irish immigrant fare—well-cooked meat, potatoes, vegetables—Sadie's baked beans were a requested dish at every family and neighborhood picnic, wake, wedding and christening for fifty years.

Mom and dad also emphasized our education, since theirs had been limited by economic demands during the Depression. Mom finished tenth grade. I still remember her reading *Treasure Island* aloud to me, complete

with pirates' accents, as a bedtime story every night over several weeks. Dad finished eighth grade. He had been a promising athlete before economics, war and bad knees intervened. He taught me a lot. I bat left, throw right because of him. Despite his best efforts, though, I wasn't going to get any athletic scholarships.

So the education my folks imposed on me was as important as it was good, first with the Sisters of Mercy. I thought at the time that the order was badly misnamed, and years later, during debates over CIA's enhanced interrogation techniques, I took pains to remind my audience that I had

Courtesy Ron Aira, Creative Services GMU.

experienced four of the techniques—two grasps and two slaps—in diocesan grade school. Still, the education was first-rate and basic. No frills.

Same at the regional Catholic high school, North Catholic. Classic parochial fare: discipline, required curriculum, theology, Latin, classic history. The whole liberal arts education. A local school, Duquesne University, was the natural choice for college: Catholic, affordable and near home. I was on active duty with America's air force before I ever sat in a classroom that didn't have a crucifix in it. I was also in the air force before I needed a car to get to school. Grade school, high school and college were all within walking distance. I have sometimes wondered if my later more global lifestyle was a reaction to those early years.

In 1967, I joined a much larger family—my military family. I was first commissioned as a second lieutenant in the air force some fifty years ago, and I served proudly alongside my sisters and brothers in uniform. I quickly learned that the line between my two families was often blurry—after all, it was my birth family that gave me the grounding, confidence and morals to join, and eventually lead, the military family. And my military family broadened my views and my experience. I not only got to meet people from all over the country, I got to serve in places that will forever affect who I am: Guam, Korea, Germany, communist Bulgaria.

In 2005, I joined yet another family, this time the good folks of the Central Intelligence Agency. I have never been part of a more dedicated, closely knit group of people, and like their military counterparts, CIA officers are willing to sacrifice not only for one another but also for our country. But they do it in secret, away from public view, unseen even by the people whose safety and security they protect.

There is also one more family that I briefly mentioned, one that pulls me back to my beloved hometown of Pittsburgh every weekend between September and January. I have considered myself a member of the Pittsburgh Steelers family for as long as I can remember, even before I started as a ball boy for the team in 1961. On Sundays, my dad and I would watch the Steelers battle it out on the grass at Forbes Field and later at Pitt Stadium.

I remember exactly where I was when the Immaculate Reception happened: on Guam, and—because Armed Forces Radio didn't carry the game live—I first heard of the catch during coverage of the second playoff game that afternoon. I didn't actually see the catch until days later, when the local Guam TV station ran a replay of the game. Unlike today, the video recording had to be flown across the Pacific. I was still on Guam and listening to games on Armed Forces Radio when we beat the Vikings for Super Bowl win number one.

What I and others took from Pittsburgh was the blue-collar ethic of the region, an ethic well captured in the words of World War II combat journalist Ernie Pyle during a 1937 visit to the city: "People here just work." For years a yellowed copy of that article has been affixed to a bulletin board at the topside station of the Monongahela Incline, one of the hillside funiculars that still service the city.

An ad campaign for the Pirates in the mid-1990s, when talent-wise they were simply awful, captured the ethic perfectly. A bare picture of home plate, a black lunch pail is dropped on it, and a voice intones, "Come out and watch a ball club that works as hard as you do." It's hard to picture the Dodgers or the Yankees with a similar theme.

I've run in several Pittsburgh Marathons since 2002. They are always great events, and running through your hometown streets to the cheers of supportive crowds is something special. But only in Pittsburgh would the crowds be offering a pierogi and think they were doing a good thing.

A recent book called *Singing the City*, an anthem to living in Pittsburgh, cited one observer who noted how blast furnaces used to turn the night sky yellow and how he pitied the poor kids in the Midwest who never saw such a sight.

The journalist Pyle summed up a similar thought nicely in 1937: "A dirty shirt collar here means prosperity."

TOM MURPHY

Thomas J. Murphy Jr. is Pittsburgh's second longest-serving mayor behind David Lawrence. The son of a steel worker, he dreamed of a new renaissance and made tough decisions to put the city on the right path that led it out of a dying age of steel mills into an era of wellness, conservation and trail development.

Growing up for me, I still remember what was there—for better or worse. I originally grew up in Greenfield, and then we moved to Baldwin, where my mother's side of the family was from Greenfield and my father's side of the family was from South Side. And with a couple of exceptions, they all worked in the steel mill…all my uncles, my grandfather, all worked in the steel mills. It was a culture, your whole life—my father was a blue-collar

...

guy, he wasn't a boss or anything—and he swung shifts every week or two, so it defined your life and the culture you grew up in. The steel mills and the companies were very paternalistic at the time and had big picnics in the summer for employees, so it permitted my family to have a good life. We were able to buy a house and a car, we could go on vacation. If we hit the numbers, we would go on a bigger vacation. So the numbers were pervasive....I can remember sitting at dinner and my parents deciding what number they were going to play for a nickel or a dime. If it hit, we would go to Geneva on the Lake or Atlantic City.

Courtesy Cade Martin.

The mills created a big social community, and if you lived on the South Side, you worked at Jones & Laughlin. And when my parents could save a little bit of money, you could move to one of the inner suburban rings like Baldwin, so it was the same whether it was Aliquippa or Homestead. So when we moved up to Baldwin, people from U.S. Steel and Mesta Machine that were all in the mills. When people would come to visit from basically Station Square, up the river for the next fifty miles along the Mon River were steel mills or major manufacturing facilities like Mesta Machine that were related to the steel industry which is hard to imagine today, so it was one solid steel mill. And I remember growing up with the pollution...every morning if you were going to use the car, you had to clean the windshield because it was covered with soot.

The mills were really the defining piece; it was about the steel mills and your church....I was raised Catholic, and church was a big part of our life. And then our family, we all lived pretty close to each other so I would see— I'm an only child—but I had four cousins my age on both sides of my family, so I would see them a couple of times a week. It was a very close-knit kind of sense of Pittsburgh.

Family and community were unifying things here, and the way we lived you typically didn't move away, which was something people underestimated about Pittsburgh and how the closing of the mills shattered those generational connections. I delivered Meals On Wheels for twenty-five years, and during my time as a legislator and as mayor, and these were people who were caught in that collapse, older people whose families had to leave to get jobs in Houston or someplace like that, so you saw the impact of the mills closing.

I was at Woodlands Seminary at first for a semester, and I don't know if I would have gone to college if I hadn't gone to the seminary—it was tempting to go to work at the steel mill. This was 1962, I'm getting out of high school, the mills were moving and you could make a great living. When you're eighteen or nineteen years old, you're going to have a pretty good paycheck. My father and most of my uncles quit school at eighth grade, they were twelve or thirteen, to work in the mill as water boys, so there was no history of going to college in my family—it was a time you didn't do that. The steel industry, it shaped our language, how steel was made and how people worked in the rolling mill, and that's how people talked about it…like it was your neighborhood.

It was a big part of growing up. So in addition to my immediate family, our friends and my parents' friends all were associated with the steel mills, people that my father worked with. So a big part of growing up for me was when my father was off he would take me to Emma's, a local neighborhood bar, and then go there and watch the baseball game, play the pinball machines. And that was my father-son outing, which I have great memories of because it was a whole community of guys who got together and had a drink in the afternoon.

If you remember South Side, when I became sixteen, I could drive—and we had one car—and my father would tell me, "You can use the car, but you have to be at that gate at midnight" to pick him up from his 4:00 p.m. to midnight shift. That's when my date was over, and I had to be at that gate. For me, that's a vivid memory because when the whistle blew, you had a huge mill with the glow, the flames and the smoke coming out of the mill and then four or five thousand men rushing out of that gate, and across Carson Street from the mill was lined with bars. There were bars across from the gate at 26th Street, so people just came rushing out, and the bars—no matter if it was twelve o'clock at night or the twelve to eight shift in the morning—the bars were five deep for a shot and a beer is what people would get. So for me, the noise, the flames and the number of people when it was dark was a great picture, was very vivid, and it's incredible that would all disappear. When I was mayor, I had the city buy the steel mill where my father worked for fifty-one years.

The other is the Hot Metal Bridge was viewed as the most strategic bridge in America during World War II because they made the hot metal—the big blast furnaces were on the Hazelwood side—and there's pictures when you came down the parkway of the blast furnace and the hot metal was carried over to the South Side to be shaped, and then it got shipped back. That bridge was guarded by the military during World War II because they were concerned that the Germans would sabotage it. I think that 20 or 25 percent of the steelmaking capacity in the United States went across that bridge every day. My father would have lunch every day sitting on that bridge; it's where he would go and talk about it. I was born in 1944. He didn't go to the service; he was seen as a critical employee working in the steel mill and would talk about it when I was growing up.

I worked in that mill during the summers, so that whole part of Pittsburgh that I remember was bars along Carson Street, and my father's family lived in a row house on Sara Street on the slopes, where, when they got more money, it was better to live in the flats.

In Pittsburgh, there was a sense of loyalty. When I got out of college, I worked for Alcoa for a number of years, and that's what you did…you went to work for a company and you would stay for fifty years. My father retired after fifty-one years with Jones & Laughlin, and he started at thirteen years old. There was that loyalty, that idea of hard work, and I saw that with my father…he came home, he was tired, he was working for eight hours a day. So I grew up with that work ethic, that sense of loyalty and that sense of community you grew up with. You get glimpses of that now, but not as much as you used to; it was something you took for granted, and when you see it you say, "Wow I'd love to have that." You see it in some neighborhoods—where people have houses not too far apart—but people are busy with things outside of their neighborhood, whereas our whole focus was our neighborhood where I grew up.

That sense of community is what always motivated me, and when my wife and I went to the Peace Corps, we were asked to help create a new little village in the middle of the jungle. It really reinforced that sense of community that led me into running a neighborhood group that I think is a really important part. So growing up Yinzer in Pittsburgh would be that sense you knew people in your neighborhood, you had that close-knit sense of community, you were part of something.

As mayor, the dominating issue for me was how do you get Pittsburghers to build a sense of community? The day that I got sworn in as mayor, it started to snow, and because I delivered Meals On Wheels for a lot years, I knew how many people were isolated. Duquesne Light was talking about roving blackouts because of the demands on electricity because it was so cold. The city was pretty well shut down, but we had city employees come to work—and Giant Eagle was an important part of this. Overnight I called up David Shapira and said, "Could you put little care packages together in your city stores?" And we called everyone over sixty-five in the city. We had our community police officers deliver these packages of bread and fruit to their homes if they needed one. We also made arrangements with Giant Eagle that if somebody needed a prescription because they were trapped in their home, we were able to get them what they needed.

So it was about that sense of community is how we thought about doing something like that…how do you get people to take care of those who need it. A sense of place, and Pittsburgh still maintains a lot of that; there was a sense of place that you felt comfortable in it, and that's what I love about Pittsburgh. For me, Greenfield, Baldwin and South Side were my *Cheers* places; it created a sense of place for me where I felt comfortable.

DAVID MOREHOUSE

David Morehouse is an American businessman who was president and chief executive officer of Pittsburgh Penguins of the National Hockey League. During his tenure, the Penguins won three Stanley Cups, reached four Stanley Cup finals and sold out every game for fourteen seasons. He previously served in politics as a member of the Clinton administration and on the presidential campaigns of Al Gore (2000) and John Kerry (2004).

I never started with any kind of dream. You know, I want to be this or I want to be that. I grew up in Beechview, which is like a hilly neighborhood between Brookline, Mount Washington and Dormont.

Where I grew up in the 1960s, as a baby boomer, I've tried to tell my kids stories, about how there were one hundred kids in my playground. I'll go through the "It's not just society has changed"; it's the sheer number of kids isn't what it used to be, when I grew up at a time where there were kids everywhere. I went from swinging on the swings and sliding down the sliding board to riding my bike around there to playing sports.

It actually traces back to my roots at Beechview's Pauline Park…I literally grew up in that playground. I spent more time there than at any other place growing up, including the eight hours in my house at night sleeping. This shaped me into who I am today, good or bad.

Brookline and Beechview were the only two neighborhoods I had exposure to.…We didn't go out much, so you had groups of kids who loafed at different parts of their neighborhood near where they live. It wouldn't be a surprise to drive down Brookline Boulevard and down Broadway Avenue with twenty to thirty teenagers standing on different corners. I don't think people have an appreciation for that. We actually stood on the corners. But a lot of what we did, a lot of what I did in this year growing up, was play sports. And we played sports in the streets.

I've traveled around the world, traveled all over the country. Nowhere I've been are people more passionate about their sports teams than Pittsburgh. This upbringing is a reflection of it. At the Penguins, we saw it when we did research. We would see the depth of interest in sports and the passion

Courtesy Pittsburgh Penguins.

people have. I think there's a sports affinity here that's deeper than it is in most other places.

One highlight of winning the Stanley Cup was taking it to the playground and the street I grew up on and seeing all of my old friends in Beechview. These people shaped who I am, and they're very grateful, but I'm saying to myself, "Where else would I take it?" This is where I grew up. These people are important to me. We've all remained friends; it keeps me centered. We all stay in touch. It's how I grew up, and I'll never forget where I came from.

One of the things that I learned there that I brought through my life, what I've learned from most Pittsburghers, is there was a hard work element as a foundation. The combination of hard work, creativity, telling it like it is, calling people out when they weren't being themselves and treating people right. I think that combination of things…made me successful in the areas I never thought I'd be successful, and it has translated in every career I've ever had.

My career path started with selling hotdogs and French fries at Hank's Dog House on West Liberty Avenue. I worked there when I was fourteen and fifteen. I was a locker room attendant at the European Health Spa at the Bigelow. I unloaded trucks at a warehouse in the North Side on Saturday mornings, at like four in the morning. But when I graduated from high school, I became a boilermaker. And when I graduated, when I graduated from high school, there weren't a lot of jobs around Pittsburgh.

I don't know what our unemployment rate was in 1978, but it was as high as it's ever been. I went to the Boilermaker union hall, and I stood in a parking lot waiting for the business agent Ironhead Galtieri to come across the street from Eat'n Park.

For a lot of people where I grew up, being a boilermaker was as good as it got. Getting that job was huge for me; it was skilled labor, and the money was pretty good. I thought I was going to be a boilermaker for the rest of my life, and that would be just fine. But when I was twenty-two, a serious accident would change everything. I was welding an I beam onto steam pipes, and a beam above snapped and headed right at me. I ducked but the beam clipped me, and getting hit in the head knocked me cold, knocked some sense into me and knocked me in a new career direction.

That accident was the worst thing that ever happened to me and it was the best thing that ever happened to me. Before the beam took me out, I'd never thought of going to college. While I was on disability, I went to community college, CCAC, then I went to Duquesne and ended up going to work for the Clinton campaign. I was a volunteer motorcade driver and ended up in the Pentagon for about a year before I worked in the White House. During that time, I always thought whatever policy position I had, I still did advance work for the president, which was traveling around the world.

So I was a kid who used to hang out at Pauline Park, and I remember laying on a ping-pong table in between basketball games, looking up at the sky, watching jets fly by and I'd never been on a plane before. I didn't fly on a plane until I was eighteen. I didn't see the ocean until I was eighteen, then here I was, once a welder who ended up getting hurt, just working my way up through a campaign hierarchy to a point where I was I was flying on Air Force One as the advance official for public appearances.

I gained confidence as I went through the different positions. I worked hard, tried to keep a modest center and treated people well.

Never much for school, I have no idea how, years later, I was accepted into and then graduated with a master's degree in public administration from the John F. Kennedy School of Government at Harvard. So I went from a welder to community college to a docket clerk working for Allegheny County to volunteering in the Clinton campaign to the Pentagon to the White House. Amazing.

It's a circuitous route that brought me back to Pittsburgh. I was the traveling chief of staff for John Kerry, and after the campaign, Penguins co-owner Ron Burkle called me. I was trying to figure out what I wanted to do next. Ron said, "You're from Pittsburgh, right? Can you go to Pittsburgh, work with the Penguins and try to find out, politically, why they haven't been able to get an arena deal done and put a strategy together to get an arena deal?" And I said sure…I thought I'd be here temporarily. We took a unique approach. Gaming was just coming online in Pennsylvania, so we partnered with a gaming company that, as part of their application program, committed to paying for a new arena for free and some community stuff around the arena. So we had kind of boxed in the other two applicants, and long story short, we got an arena deal done.

At the end of the day, I don't see a big difference between me and the kids I grew up with that didn't stand in front of the Boilermaker Hall and get a job and ended up underemployed for most of their lives because they graduated when steel industry collapsed. There wasn't much of a difference between me and those kids. I just feel like I got lucky and I made good decisions when I had decision points. But for some reason, you know, I was in the right place at the right time. The values I learned growing up in Beechview propelled me to an opportunity where when I had a decision to make, I was able to make the decision that sent me in the right direction. That's the only difference.

SPORTS

BILL COWHER

William Laird Cowher is an American sports analyst, former football player and coach. Following a six-year playing career as a linebacker in the National Football League, he served as a head coach in the NFL for fifteen seasons with the Pittsburgh Steelers. At the age of thirty-four, Cowher succeeded legendary Hall of Fame coach Chuck Noll and won Super Bowl XL in 2005.

I think every time my wife and I come back to Pittsburgh, I feel like nothing has changed—time has stood still. At the same time, I say that in a very complimentary way, and it becomes moments of reflection. I have two brothers there, so we always come back, have dinner at il Pizzaiolo, one block from where my mom and dad lived in Mount Lebanon, even though they both have passed on. I like to kick off our time with family—you come back to Pittsburgh for family.

When we're there, it's memories. The last trip, we went to Kennywood so my six grandkids could experience Kennywood for the first time. I went on the Jack Rabbit with one of them; it was the very first roller coaster he was ever on. Those are special moments, what you grew up with, and I go back to the days when I would ask people for extra tickets because you had to get extra tickets if you wanted to stay longer.

We ended up going to a Pirates game, which used to be Forbes Field, now it's PNC Park, so things have modernized to a large degree but they really haven't changed. It's the same atmosphere, the same people, the same make-up and the same feeling and experience. I want my grandkids to experience that. My daughters have experienced that, so it's a generational thing that you want to do. I grew up there, I gave it to my kids when I came back to coach. They were in the same house for fifteen years, went to Fox Chapel High School and now they're bringing their kids back, so it's generation to generation to the next generation. To me, that's what you do as a Pittsburgher—you pass on what's great about the city.

Courtesy ESPN.

I grew up in Crafton. We moved from Beechview when I was seven or eight years old, where my dad was an auditor for Ohio Casualty Insurance Company, and he was great with numbers. I had a paper route from nine years old, me and my brother. I worked in the steel mills; I worked in a nursery. I was blessed to be able to have fun playing football for the Crafton Little Cougars, walking down to the athletic field with my shoulder pads on and holding my helmet. That's how I went to practice, I walked down and walked back, a couple of miles. You grew up there with just very simple ideas.

My takeaway is my father taught me three things: commitment—never quit because if you quit once you'll quit again, so he never allowed me to start something and not finish it; your work ethic—you have to work harder than the other person; and self-confidence—don't be intimidated by anyone or anything. He was a guy who inbred those things in me. He grew up in Belle Vernon, and my mom was from Pittsburgh as well, so it was one of those things to me was being very proud being from there; it was about work ethic, competing, about winning, particularly in the '70s, when the Steelers won Super Bowls.

I graduated from high school in 1975, went to college and played at NC State. Then to come back to Pittsburgh at age thirty-four and be the head coach of your hometown team was pretty special.

As a kid, and why I love going back to Pittsburgh, is the normality to it. I had a summer job; I saved money to spend it in a certain way. I loved competing, playing football and basketball....I had two brothers, and I enjoyed the elements of community. We're all from Pittsburgh, but there are different parts of Pittsburgh competing against Pittsburgh. There was a degree of pride that you had depending on where you were from. If you were from Carnegie you were a certain way and if you were from Crafton you were a certain way, but we merged together to form Carlynton High School in my eighth grade. I was part of the fourth graduating class, so we really grew together. There were battles—there was Crafton versus Carnegie versus Roslyn Farms—and you identified with each one of them. I grew up in that era where I played against Marvin Lewis at Fort Cherry. And I went to the IUP football camp, and we had four or five guys from Carlynton and he had four or five guys from Fort Cherry. We talked about we'll see who wins that game in September. Winning was everything from that standpoint, but it was only because of what you represented as your community.

My parents were the biggest influencers in my life because they never missed a game, even when I was at NC State. They would drive down from Pittsburgh on Saturday, and they would get up at like five o'clock because my dad had to be back for the Steelers game. They came to every basketball game that I played in, so they were the most influential. I had some great midget football coaches like Dick Meyer when I was playing for the Crafton Little Cougars and Ed Hammer—two guys that I remember to this day. Bill Yost, my high school coach, the time he spent with me to teach me how to long snap. And I would go to these camps, the Mountain State Achievement Camp when Jim Carlen was the coach at West Virginia, then it became the Mountaineer Football Camp when a guy named Bobby Bowden took over. My dad would drop me off down there when I was the youngest kid in camp and pick me up a week later.

Then I would go to Red Manning's basketball camp. My dad went to Duquesne, so I would go to the Civic Arena to watch them on Sunday afternoons. I loved basketball, and I loved Duquesne when they had the Nelson Twins, Jarrett Durham, Mickey Davis, Billy Zopf and Moe Barr. I would go to Forbes Field to watch the Pirates, but I never went to many football games at Three Rivers Stadium. Most of the time it was watching the Steelers on TV or listening to them on the radio like my dad did. Sports were everything, and when the Pirates and Steelers both won in '79—what that did for the city, particularly the hard work and steel mill ethic, was inspirational.

That was your identity because that's where you were from. For me, Pittsburgh has always been about work ethic, humility, never forgetting where you came from, that there were always people who helped you along the way, it isn't always about you and taking pride in what you do. How many times did I hear from Mr. Rooney: "Coach, do the right thing," and he would walk out of the room. I would find myself saying, "You grew up here. You know what the right thing is for Pittsburgh. Get back up. And don't let history dictate your future."

There's no greater motivation in life than when somebody says, "You probably can't do this." That's all I needed to hear. "You're just a bunch of steel workers." And what did they all have in common: they love to compete, there is humility in what they do and there's a lot of pride in what they do. They'll find a way to get it done, and the bottom line is they're winners. Winners doesn't mean you'll have a winning record every time, but you go about things in a manner in which you're proud and you love to compete.

Pittsburghers never get complacent…they are afraid to fail. I was motivated by the fear of failure more than being motivated by the joy of succeeding. When I got the Steelers head coaching job in 1992, the first thing I said was, "You know, if I don't screw this up I can go back to my twentieth high school reunion as the head coach of my hometown team." So my first goal was to just not get fired. Then every year to be better than the year before…it's the same way with TV. It's what growth is all about.

Even though my life has changed in many ways, I really haven't changed. I enjoyed writing the book that I did that allowed me to reflect on my upbringing and the people that were an influence on my life, being grateful for all the opportunities that were given to me. The attributes that my parents taught me I can never give back to them. Pittsburgh taught me the value of things like hard work, and those things have never left me.

DICK GROAT

Dick Groat, a native of Wilkinsburg, spent nine of his fourteen seasons as a major-league shortstop with the Pittsburgh Pirates and won the National League MVP award in 1960. A two-sport athlete at Duke University, Groat was a two-time All-American in baseball and basketball and briefly juggled professional baseball and basketball careers before committing himself to the diamond full time.

My family made me whatever I might be. I had great parents and two sisters that were schoolteachers and two brothers who were athletes at Pitt.

Courtesy Associated Press.

I was a very fortunate person to have grown up as the baby in the family. There was like sixteen years' difference between my older brothers and sisters and myself.

Baseball and basketball was my whole life in those days. I never really played any organized baseball. There was no such thing as Little League or Pony League back then. I played probably twenty times more basketball than I did baseball. You played on the playgrounds in summer; you never had anything organized. But you always had a game. Something you don't see today. Now you can drive by all kinds of fields and playgrounds and never see a pick-up game. It seems that unless the kids have a uniform and an umpire they don't play baseball anymore. You see kids playing basketball on playgrounds, but the philosophy when we grew up was we learned to play the game because of our peers. When we were young, if you didn't do the job they didn't pick you the next time.

That's the way it was when we were growing up. Everybody wanted to play; you could not wait to get out there and play the baseball or softball game that evening. We played all day and then we wanted to play with the big guys in the evening, and that's how we learned to play the game. My first organized baseball experience was when I was a sophomore in high school, and then I played American Legion baseball one summer. I always said I was the luckiest guy in the world, to have grown up in this area where everything seemed to fall into place for me—that's how fortunate I was.

I was very willing to pay the price to spend more time on the practice facility than any other player, whether it be a Duke University or Swissvale High School or with the Pirates. It's the way I believed, the way I felt. I can remember certain basketball games over and over and over again, and when I'd miss a few shots, I'd say, "You're never going to be All-American that way."

I got a basketball scholarship to Duke University. I signed with the Pirates during my last semester with Duke, so I played with them during the summer of 1952. Branch Rickey treated me really well, and he agreed that he would give me the chance to play in the big leagues. I was also drafted in the NBA and played professional basketball while I finished my degree at Duke. Then I spent two years in the army. I returned and played the 1955 season with the

Pirates and continued to play another fourteen years. My teammate Jerry Lynch and I decided to build a golf course, Champion Lakes in Ligonier, and my daughter and I are still here running it more than fifty years later.

I was intimidated at first. I never felt that way in basketball because I was much better at it, so this was kind of new. I remember everything about my first at bat though. I was facing Jim Hearn, and I took the first pitch because I was shaking like a leaf. I stepped out of the batter's box and wondered what I was doing there. Then he threw me a slow pitch, and I hit it right back to the mound. After the game, the manager told me to get my rest because I was going to be in the lineup the next day.

Mr. Rickey made the decision to give up basketball for me. I had a five-year contract with the Pirates, and when I came back from the service I went right to baseball. I was ready to go back to the Pistons because I thought I could do that for a few years since I was making more money, but Rickey said I couldn't do that. If I had one disappointment in my life, it would be that I wasn't able to play basketball for at least a few more years.

The Pirates were such a bad baseball team in the early years, but then we grew up and came in second in 1958 and we all just kept improving together. We became a very strong ball club, and we had learned how to win. When the 1960 World Series came around, I was coming off a broken wrist and had only played two games before the series. The wrist was not where I would have liked it to be, so I couldn't open my glove all the way, but obviously it ended up working out for us.

I was heartbroken to hear that I had been traded. Pittsburgh is my hometown, and I never wanted to leave. It's the greatest city in the world, and I never wanted to leave. That was one of the toughest winters that I've ever spent, but I had the best year of my career in 1963 with the Cardinals. I hit in front of Stan Musial the whole season, and I had never seen so many good pitches to hit.

I've been very fortunate. We beat the Yankees twice for the World Series for one thing. I was able to play professional basketball, which was my first love and my best sport at least for one year. Because of that and my Pirate background, I've broadcasted basketball for the University of Pittsburgh with the best broadcaster anywhere, Bill Hillgrove.

I could have never pictured myself becoming a broadcaster, but thank God that it happened because it's an absolute joy to me and I've loved every minute of it. I love college basketball. It was my first love. And just being around all of the kids keeps me young. Every day that I walked into a basketball arena is a joy to me.

I feel like I'm getting older. I know I can't play golf any longer because I've lost my equilibrium, but other than that I feel fine and all I can say is life has been extremely good to me.

JIM KELLY

Jim Kelly grew up in East Brady, a small Western Pennsylvania town nestled along the Allegheny River, and was the quarterback for the Buffalo Bills from 1986 to 1996. In addition to four Super Bowl appearances (XXV–XXVIII), he was elected in 2002 to the Pro Football Hall of Fame. In 1987, Jim established the Kelly for Kids Foundation (KFK), which has raised more than $1 million for children's charities in Western New York.

It all started with my mother and father, who was raised in an orphanage in Pittsburgh, and they decided to have children and wound up with six boys in Millvale. When my dad was transferred to the small town of East Brady, Pennsylvania, I started in second grade, and from there everything blossomed. Growing up a Steelers fan, watching [Terry] Bradshaw, loving those days. I later got to know a lot of those guys that I looked up to when I was just a little boy, but East Brady was the key with my father and my best friend and high school football coach Terry Henry.

I am so proud to be from East Brady, Pennsylvania. For a small-town country boy to make it where I am and be able to share all I've accomplished with my hometown buds, and still see my high school coach, I'm honored. The mentality was you wanted to be the best, not just in football or basketball, but I always wanted to do well for one reason and that was to make my mom and dad proud and my brothers proud.

Courtesy ESPN.

For me, it's about family. Western Pennsylvania has always been family. East Brady's always been my home. I'm sixty-two now and I have the closest family you could possibly have. I am so blessed to have the family and the community I grew up in. I still go back every single year, and for me it is fun. That's what my goal was; not sure what the situation was going to be in my future, but I had big dreams and you never know. I worked hard enough. Thank God it all came to the forefront, and I wound up fulfilling a lot of dreams.

In my backyard, playing sports was all we did. I played basketball, football, golf—I did it all. I wore no. 12 that I put on with a magic marker. Growing up near Pittsburgh, I was a big Terry Bradshaw fan on the field. And then, off the field, I wanted to be like Joe Namath. I think everybody did back in those days.

To be honest with you, where I'm from, you're either a Pitt or Penn State fan. And I've always been a Penn State fan, always loved Joe Paterno and always wanted to play for the Nittany Lions.

I went to Paterno's football camp my junior and senior years of high school, thinking I showed him enough that I could play the position of quarterback. But unfortunately for me, I guess I should say unfortunately for Penn State, he recruited me as a linebacker. Later on, he called me and he said, "We've already signed two all-state quarterbacks, but we'll give you a scholarship as a linebacker."

Of course, the first thing I did was…I have three older brothers…I called my oldest brother, Pat, who played in the NFL with the Baltimore Colts. What do you think I should do? And he said, "Brother, I have a few words of advice for you. Before you board those chartered flights for the away games, the flight attendants never want to know who the linebackers are. They always want to know who's the quarterback." I said that's enough for me.…I'm a quarterback, and the rest is history. I went on to the University of Miami and had a great, great time.

Growing up in Western Pennsylvania, growing up with the work ethic that I had, the toughness that I had to have, you were either tough or you would be thrown to the side. The toughness part came from that, but when I had my son, who was born on my birthday, Valentine's Day, when he was diagnosed with his fatal disease, I saw what toughness was all about. When they talk about Kelly Tough through all my cancer battles, my toughness came from my son. Watching him for those eight and a half years, watching how he fought through every single pain that he had, and to see what he went through, nothing touched what he went through.

I knew when I started my cancer battle that I was doing it for my little boy, and I know he helped me get there. I was very blessed, and I know why the good Lord put me in the situation that I'm in now. I may have lost four Super Bowls, but I kicked cancer's ass four times. It was because of the toughness my son showed me and the toughness my father brought us up to be.

I've had many roller coaster rides and ups-and-downs in my life, but now what I do for a living is I travel speaking. That's the platform I was given to be able to be a difference maker for other people who are looking to give up….I'm trying to make people understand that they can be the difference maker. You don't have to be a pro quarterback or a celebrity. You can be a normal person working nine to five; you can be that difference maker…a spouse, a friend, a sibling. That's what it's all about.

JOHN CALIPARI

A players-first coach with a penchant for helping people reach their dreams, John Calipari, a Naismith Memorial Basketball Hall of Famer, has guided six teams to the college basketball Final Four, led one to a national championship in 2012 and helped fifty-six players earn selection in the NBA draft during his thirty-one-year college coaching career. In addition, the Calipari Foundation has raised millions of dollars to help the lives of those in need in Kentucky, Pittsburgh and across the country. During his time as the head coach at Kentucky, he's helped raise more than $10 million to aid in natural disaster relief in places like Haiti, Houston and the state of Kentucky. He lives by the motto that "It's never a matter of how far you have fallen, but instead it's about how high you bounce back."

We didn't have much growing up, but our parents had expectations that we could go on to college. We all did, although our parents had only a high school education. My dad worked at the Greater Pittsburgh Airport as a baggage handler, and my mom worked at the cafeteria. My house was a mile from that airport, grew up in Moon Township, in that bedroom community where we all grew up the same. No one ever locked the door, no one called with play dates, you just went over to someone else's house. And we were all raised by somebody else's mother.

Our dads were laborers, working double shifts, working Friday to Friday, getting paid on Friday. In between, Saturday, Sunday and Monday were pretty good days with the food. Tuesday got a little lighter, Wednesday and Thursday were tough. Thursday was breakfast for dinner. But no one knew

Courtesy University of Kentucky.

that anyone lived any differently. There weren't bank presidents where I grew up. The only professionals in our lives were the teachers. We didn't know any other professionals. So all I wanted to be was a high school coach and teacher. I majored in business and marketing in case it didn't work out.

My dad was more grind, work, keep it rolling. My mom was more dream big, nothing holds you back. I miss her spirit, her positive energy. She wouldn't let anybody steal her joy. Her whole thing was, "You keep doing right, having a good heart, treat people right and you'll be fine." Just keep marching and moving.

I'm the same guy I've always been. My heart's the same. My friends are the same. My approach to things is the same. I'm white-privileged, even though I grew up the way I grew up. I was still white, which means I had an advantage. I had one pair of tennis shoes, but that didn't matter. People took pride in their neighborhood, took pride in their community. And each community was its own community. Someone would say, "I grew up on the north side, or Squirrel Hill," and be proud of that.

It was my mother who made sure that my two sisters, Terri and Lea, and I kept shooting for the stars. The biggest thing was she taught us to dream beyond our surroundings. She said, "Look, around. This doesn't hold you back. Just because this is how it is right now, it doesn't have to be that way for you." When I was growing up, her goal was for us to be college-educated, and she wanted us to live in a $100,000 house. The house we grew up in was $16,000, and the mortgage was $63 a month.

When I got my first head coaching position and I'm ready to buy my first house, it's in Massachusetts, 1988. The realtor says, "How much do you want to spend?" What do you think I said? $100,000. I said I want to spend $100,000. There was a garage. I waved the lady on. I said, "Keep going." We ended up having to pay $163,000. I was like, "We better win some games, honey. We better have a big camp. You better keep making those clothes." The house cost $163,000, but it was in the mountains because it was over $200,000 near the campus, which I could have never afforded. What was my salary? I think it was $63,000. We were up in Shutesbury, fifteen miles in the mountains. It used to snow up there more than it did in Amherst. Those were the good old times.

My mom loved that house. It was a different time. We would play in New York City and be in the Marriott Marquis in the corner suite and my dad would walk in and look at the back of the door. "Pfft, $600." His mortgage was $63 a month, and he sees $600 a night. He said, "Son, I don't know what you're doing, keep fooling them though."

I grew up in football country, and it always will be, but good basketball has been played there. Herb Sendek coached, Sean Miller, Ryan Miller. You're talking major college coaches. Then locally you had Doc Zeke at Beaver, Vic Bianchi at Ambridge, Frank Chan at Beaver Falls, John Miller first at Ellwood City then Blackhawk, my coach Bill Sacco—these guys were bigger than life. Good coaching. We didn't grow up in an era of AAU basketball though. Ours was pickup basketball. You got in the car and you went to wherever everybody would be playing. Whether it was in Monaca, whether it was in Center Township. Jump in the car, go to Beaver, go to Midland and see where everybody was playing on different days. Different time and era.

Today, I'm still close with that group of guys. They'll come down to a game, and we play cards in my house, twelve of us. You forge relationships that are lifelong when we're all in the same boat, and everybody enjoys doing it so you can travel with a bunch of guys. You can leave Pittsburgh, but it's not leaving you. When I come back home, I still enjoy the Sicilian square pizza. I'll go to Police Station Pizza in Ambridge and sit on the stoop having a pizza, just like we used to.

As I get older, you start changing how you feel. I'm telling you, when I was thirty-five and forty, I'm like how do guys do it, twenty more years? I'm in the locker room ten minutes before a game I know we have very little chance of winning, or a game we should win or a big game. Oh my gosh, I'm thinking, "How do people do this twenty years?" As you get older, and I've been fortunate enough to get old in this position of coaching, I've been blessed in so many ways. All I can tell you is I think I got a contract for a long time. As long as I'm helping kids and kids are doing the things they're doing and they're elevating the program academically, with wins, more Final Fours, league championships, I'm not going to change. It's going to be about these kids. *No one* is stealing my joy.

SUZIE McCONNELL-SERIO

Suzie McConnell-Serio is a women's basketball coach, player and Olympic athlete. A proven winner at every level, McConnell-Serio was named the best five-foot-four basketball player, male or female, of all time by Sports Illustrated. *McConnell-Serio was inducted into the Women's Basketball Hall of Fame and the Western Pennsylvania Sports Hall of Fame. She has been honored as a* USA Today *All-Time Women's Basketball Team selection and as one of the* Sports Illustrated *Top 50 Pennsylvania Athletes of the Century.*

I played basketball all over the world, from nearby Gund Arena as a member of the WNBA's Cleveland Rockers to Seoul, South Korea, as a gold medalist in the 1988 Olympic Games. But I started, in the 1970s, shooting at the court at Moore Park in Brookline, very close to downtown Pittsburgh; it was a five-minute drive.

We were just outside as much as we could be, playing sports. It could be playing wiffle ball in the street, NERF football....We used to play a huge game of release with all of the neighborhood kids. We would play outside until dinnertime, eat quickly and then we'd be out playing until it was dark.

Growing up in Brookline and my family are everything to me. It helped me become the person and accomplish things that I've accomplished. To this day, I'm still very close with my family. But growing up in a big family, obviously, a basketball family, sports-oriented family, we competed with everything. We always had people to play any sport with, out in the street, in our backyard. We had a basketball hoop up against the chimney—we would play until it was dark. Then finally my father put up a spotlight so we could play even through the dark...all of a sudden, the court was lit up. It was like we had a whole new court. It was just a lot of fun, but it also made me the competitor I am being a part of a family like mine.

My older brothers are the two that I looked up to the most because I had the opportunity to learn from them firsthand, growing up with them, watching them play, living in the in the same house as them. And it was funny because when I say we always had people to play games with, it was always my oldest brother, Tom, with my sister Kathy who's a year younger and then it was myself and Tim were teammates. And we would play everything from wiffle ball to NERF football to basketball. Whether it was in the snow or with summer sunshine, we had a lot of great matches and a great game, playing two on two in every sport.

I grew up being at Moore Park on a daily basis and then also played baseball and softball at the Brooklyn Community Center. The grade school

Courtesy University of Pittsburgh.

Our Lady of Loreto didn't have a gym, and we would practice during the week and play our games on Sunday at the Brooklyn Community Center. So Moore Park and Brooklyn Community Center were a big part of my childhood growing up.

We didn't have a girls' team, so I started showing up to the boys' practice. I would shoot on the side and do some of the drills with them. I had thirty-two in my graduating class in eighth grade. It was a small Catholic school, we were taught by nuns—it was just what we knew. I loved it though. It was intimate; class sizes were small.

Pittsburgh has always been home for us even though I lived for brief periods in other cities, and Pittsburgh is about family. It's about the community. We just think Pittsburgh is a great city, and we're proud to be a part of it.

I depended on family to not only help me with my training when I was in college trying to make the U.S. Olympic team. But I was also dependent on my sister, my parents and my husband in helping take care of my children. So it was definitely a family effort when I was trying to do the things that I've done after having a fourth child coming back to play in the WNBA. And my husband, Pete, was taking care of three daughters that are ages one, two and three and my son was seven. He would take care of them all summer when I was training, and we moved our family to Minnesota for three years when I was coaching in the WNBA with the Minnesota Lynx. So he's made some sacrifices as well to allow me to have those opportunities in my career.

When we were in Minnesota, it was an easy decision for us to move back home. We brought our kids back home, where they're surrounded by family and friends, back into the same school district and Upper St. Clair. It was an easy decision for us to come back and raise a family here and just be a part of the community. This is a great place. And, you know, we love it here.

Even as I began playing at Seton-LaSalle Catholic High School, I didn't yet realize how prominent basketball would become in my life. Things changed when I participated in national youth tournaments with the Amateur Athletic Union, or AAU—still a critical step in the development of young players today, but even more prominent then when there weren't all of these tournaments all over the country. Then the recruiting started. That's when, I guess, I really started thinking I would play in college.

Growing up, even in college and just out of college, I never envisioned myself coaching. My degree is in secondary education, so I thought I would teach but I never really thought that I would get into coaching. It was Fran Mannion, who was the athletic director at Oakland Catholic, that reached out to me. I was young, twenty-four years old and pregnant with my first child. I was pleasantly surprised that he reached out, and after I thought about it, I determined it was my way of getting back into the game of basketball, and hopefully, helping young girls have some of the opportunities, some of the experiences that I was very fortunate to have.

From day one, I was hooked. I was consumed with it. The game had always been a big part of my life as a player and then even more so as a coach because so much more goes into coaching than being a player as far as planning, preparing practices, games. It was something I truly enjoyed. I was at Oakland Catholic for thirteen years and built some incredible memories with so many players that I've had the opportunity to coach and keep in touch with.

I was with Duquesne University for six years, then moved to Pitt, where I was with my sister for five years. We played together through elementary school up through high school, then I went to Penn State, she went to Virginia. She was in the WNBA for two years with the Tulsa Shock and at that point had been away from home for so long. When I got the Pitt job, it was something we had talked about bringing her back home and having the opportunity to coach together. She wanted to move back to Pittsburgh, bring her family back here, have her children grow up around their cousins, be around our parents and be around family. And I loved it…she's been my best friend basically growing up my entire life, and to have the opportunity to work with her was special for me.

I was out of coaching for a year after Pitt, and for the last four I've been helping my husband, Pete, coach the Upper St. Clair girls. So, in my life, my coaching career has gone full circle. I started out in high school, and here I am back in. And I just love coaching again. You know, when he asked me to be an assistant four years ago, and he was looking for someone, it was just an opportunity to help him. And I truly love being on the court with the players.

Teaching them the game, watching them progress with player development and then seeing them transfer that into game situation. So it's been exciting to be back on the court coaching again.

I just think growing up in Pittsburgh, it's a blue-collar town. It's a sports town. You're a fan of the professional sports teams here. No matter where you live, no matter how old you are. I wouldn't trade growing up in Pittsburgh, and in particular Brookline, for anything because I had the opportunity to experience so many different things especially through the game of basketball, and getting an early start playing on the boys team for two years. I'm thankful to Dan Kail for the opportunity—he coached every one of us in our family—but he's the one who got me started in basketball. And then my two brothers. But I look back on what I was able to experience and things I was able to do throughout my life, and I believe it's a direct result of growing up in Pittsburgh and being a part of an outstanding family.

I don't know what it's like growing up somewhere else, but the first thing we did when things didn't work out for me in Minnesota, we moved back to Pittsburgh. We're all about family. It's where my parents chose to live, where we grew up and then all of my siblings live in Pittsburgh. We are all here, and again, family is everything.

SWIN CASH

Swin Cash was born in the Pittsburgh suburb of McKeesport and raised by her mother, Cynthia. Cash attended McKeesport Area High School, where she participated in the WBCA High School All-America Game and earned MVP honors. Known for her passion on the court, Cash earned an enviable cache of awards: two college NCAA championships at the University of Connecticut while being named the 2002 Final Four's Most Outstanding Player, three WNBA championships, two Olympic gold medals for USA Basketball and even a coveted spot on a Wheaties box. She currently serves as the vice-president of Basketball Operations and Team Development for the New Orleans Pelicans of the National Basketball Association. Off the court, Cash is the founder of Cash Building Blocks, which is an urban development company that renovates and offers affordable homes for low-income families, and is the founder of Cash for Kids, which provides after-school programs for children in McKeesport and Allegheny County.

You may look at me and see a polished woman today, but I promise you I'm the product of God's grace, prayer, hard work and mental toughness. That was formed growing up in McKeesport, where my foundation was my family and watching my mom daily. I was just raised that way. My mom is one of fourteen; I have like seventy-five first cousins. We're a big family; we're a big sports family. It's impossible to grow up in the Pittsburgh area and not be connected through sports somehow, and that was part of our DNA.

I think if you just look at how I've been throughout my career, I live the mantra and the scripture, "To whom much is given, much is required." And I feel it's pivotal that other female athletes, male athletes as well, you're given this platform and you want to make sure that you can maximize it to its potential. I not only see myself in some of these young female athletes, but now as a parent of two young boys, I see myself from a parent's standpoint of kids needing resources, of kids needing apparel and equipment because they're going to be involved in sports and how this game is going to directly affect the pockets of their parents. So I see it from a different view now being older and being a mom, but I also was able to see it just being a young athlete who grew up in humble beginnings in McKeesport who didn't always have the means to buy a lot of the things that were needed and people stepped up to the plate to also help me and inspire me along the way.

A lot of times you hear those stories where they say, "Oh, God, it was so hard." Yes, I came from the projects. I didn't have this. I didn't know what I didn't have when I was younger. But what I knew is that everybody—from the guys on the street corner selling drugs to the older woman who was friends with my grandpa—contributed to being like, "This kid is passionate about something, so we want to try and help her." I never forgot that.

One of the things that kept coming to my mind is that life is like a bridge. You start out on one side, you never know what obstacles and things are on that side, but you're always trying to push to get to the other side. And I think my life has been like that. Pittsburgh has so many bridges, so as I kept walking I kept thinking, "You're always going to come to a situation where there's a bridge in your life, and you can make the decision, either fight to get over it, or are you going to stay put?"

I dealt with a lot of situations a lot of kids deal with today—the crime rate, being slighted in certain ways where you don't have as many opportunities as other kids. I was talented with basketball, but my hustle was everything else. My goal with basketball wasn't just to be in the WNBA or go to the Olympics; my goal was to get an education because I knew my education meant I'm going to be successful. So if you're trying to get over that bridge, what's your hustle? Find your hustle. We all got a hustle. I used sports as my hustle.

Courtesy Layne Murdoch.

One of my mentors is my "Paps," I call him. His name is Bob Gallagher, and he was a huge influence in my life in how he was able to give back to me. I was living in McKeesport public housing, and he was a mentor in my life since I was thirteen. He never asked our family for one thing. He just cared about how he could help us through the process. I remember when he dropped me off at UConn with my mom and my godmother, and everybody kind of looked at him funny because he was an older white man who I called my "Paps" and considered a member of the family. He's been a significant figure throughout my life that I really cherish. I would say my entire family as well. I have a really big family, but they always saw something special in me, and they always made sure I stayed on the right path. That old saying goes, "It takes a village to raise a child." Well, I definitely had that village around me.

The community support I received to pursue my dreams has motivated me to help people back home. That's a primary reason why, in 2005, I started Cash for Kids, a nonprofit designed to motivate, educate and elevate kids. More than two thousand kids in McKeesport and across the country have been impacted by the organization. People think of just the financial gifts you give, but it's also your time. I think that matters just as much. Some of these young girls who may not even know about my playing career, they're going to now be able to go back and say, "Hey, I talked to Swin Cash," and because of the resources we have they can go on the internet and look at the things I've done and understand what it meant today to have that time to talk and ask questions to help them along the way.

Hopefully, these young girls see pathways I didn't see. Pull from the game what I couldn't. And then pour back into the game more than I have. I was always a fighter. I always used people's negative energy as motivation of why I couldn't achieve something, to do it. Sue Bird and I always used to have this saying: "The one thing they can't take away from you is winning, so just go win. Period."

Whenever I get the opportunity to come back home, I do. The one thing I appreciate about Pittsburgh is when you come through those tunnels and you see the city, your heart just feels like it's home, and you know exactly where you're driving and what direction your heading in.

For me, heading back to McKeesport is always coming through those tunnels, and I'm going to see my mom, this family member, my cousin, and it makes you feel good. I want to be able to help young people know that if they work hard enough, good things can happen to them, just like good things have happened to me.

TONY DORSETT

Running back Tony Dorsett was one of the more gifted tailbacks in the history of football, an All-American Heisman Trophy–winning running back at the University of Pittsburgh and a National Football League Hall of Famer for the Dallas Cowboys and Denver Broncos.

It all started with my four older brothers who were exceptional athletes, especially football players. I wasn't all that concerned about athletics as a little kid. I would play in the neighborhood and down at the playground, but I wasn't in tune with like Pop Warner football. One day I went with my brother to his football practice, and I saw him getting hit and I thought, "Whoa, I don't want to play football, I don't want to play this game." Eventually, I grew out of some of that scariness and ended up playing football.

The blue-collar attitude that was in Western Pennsylvania is legendary. Everyone in my neighborhood worked in a steel mill, and it was quite interesting. One day I went down to the mill's open-hearth department to meet my dad to get his car keys because I had some things to do. I saw this man walking toward me in my direction. It looked like my dad, the way he walks, but he was covered in filth with a mask of grime. That experience that day got me to the point where I said I have to get my education. And my dad told me, "If you come in the mill, you don't know if you're coming out. And if you do, you might be missing an arm or eye or

Courtesy Heisman Trophy Trust.

leg. Do something better with your life." That hit me like a ton of bricks, and I made my mind up that I was going to go to college.

As a young man, I was very introverted, quiet and shy, and I didn't trust a lot of people. When I was being recruited, all of these coaches were making promises about what they were going to do for my family and myself. It wasn't what I was looking for. I decided that I wanted to go to school someplace close so my family can come and watch me play. That helped me decide to play college football at the University of Pittsburgh.

From being a young boy watching my dad work in a Pennsylvania steel mill, vowing to never work there myself, to my momma's homemade pies, I came to the University of Pittsburgh a young boy, left a young man and it was because of the university, both on and off the field, that has made my life special.

It wasn't easy for me though. I was one of only a handful of Blacks among more than 1,500 Hopewell students, living in two worlds: by night a resident of the Hill, hardscrabble and all Black, and by day a student at a nearly all-white high school.

Jackie Sherrill was doing the recruiting, and every day at school I would see his car. They didn't want Penn State to recruit me because after my last high school game, the *Beaver County Times* ran a headline that said, "Penn State Next Stop."

I wanted to be close to my mother and my family, so my first year at Pitt I spent more time at home than I did on campus. I would come downstairs from my room into the dorm lobby, and they heard about me or would see me on the field, but they didn't know who I was because I was really, really, really shy. When I started getting all of that publicity, I wasn't quite ready for it. For the first time, I was on my own and didn't want the limelight.

I have a lot of pride in where I went to school. Not only that, but this is where I was born and raised. This is Aliquippa and Pittsburgh. This is me. This is where I got everything. So when I get a chance to come back, it's twofold: I get to come back to my alma mater and I also get to see my family and friends. Whenever I get a chance to support my university, I'm more than happy and willing to do it.

Little things make big things happen. Those are words I lived by all the way through college and later the NFL, and still do today. Football is a game that you can learn a lot of life lessons in. Football comes and goes, but those lessons live forever. You've got to do the little things, and that's what I try to do.

My dad was not an educated man, but he would tell me, "Son, you've got to get your education," and he said the same things Johnny Majors said:

"You get out of it what you put into it. If you want to work hard you'll get results. If you put in the work, you can expect great things."

For me, when I came to the NFL, I thought if I could make it five years I would be thrilled. Well, I doubled that and some change.

When you're a kid growing up in Western Pennsylvania, you know steel, where my father earned a living in J&L Steel in Aliquippa, and you know the Steelers. When I was a kid, I always wanted to wear the black and gold. Fortunately for me, I ended up here in Dallas in silver and blue. The Steelers just happen to be my 1B team. The Cowboys are 1A.

DAN MARINO

Dan Marino was a nine-time Pro Bowl quarterback in the National Football League for seventeen seasons with the Miami Dolphins after a successful college career at the University of Pittsburgh, where he was named first-team All-American. He established the Dan Marino Foundation in 1992 with his wife, Claire, after their son was diagnosed with autism. The foundation has distributed tens of millions of dollars to research, services and treatment programs serving children with neurodevelopmental disabilities.

As a young man, God blessed me with a special talent to throw a football, and I was very fortunate to grow up in an environment like the city of Pittsburgh, in the neighborhood of Oakland, an area that was full of football tradition. My dream started right there on Parkview Avenue, and it stayed there for twenty-one years. There are not many players who can say they went to grade school, high school, college all in the same neighborhood, all within a short walk from the home that I grew up in. I might be the only one. I was blessed, and it was literally a ten-minute walk from my home to the fifty-yard line of old Pitt Stadium.

I lived right across the street from the church when I was a kid, and I still have vivid memories of playing football for St. Regis. On the morning of games, we would go to church in full dress uniform. We'd have cleats, pads, helmets, everything. We were wearing everything, and the coaches would lead us in prayer. We would say Hail Marys and Our Fathers in praying for victory, and then we'd march down the street, cheerleaders, band playing, to play our game. It didn't get much better than that. And you know what? We never lost.

I've always been a quarterback. Well, almost always. At St. Regis, sometimes I was a wide receiver when another kid, Joe Carcia, was the quarterback, but

Courtesy Sports Illustrated.

I was the quarterback most of the time. I could always throw. Bigger guys could throw better than me as a kid because they were just bigger guys.

It was such a big deal for me to attend Central Catholic, but I didn't know I was going to be a professional athlete. I didn't know I was going to be in the Hall of Fame. I always dreamt about it. And, you know what, I did it. So don't let anybody tell you can't be what you want to be in life.

From Central Catholic, I went right down Fifth Avenue a few blocks to the University of Pittsburgh, where I had four great years. Pitt taught me how to compete at a high level. To tell you how talented our teams were, most weeks our practices were tougher and more demanding than any games we'd play on Saturday. I still say the 1980 team could've beat Georgia at one o'clock, Notre Dame at four o'clock and been national champs if we were only given the chance. I have friends like Rickey Jackson, Hugh Green, Jimbo Covert—they'd all attest to that and I still believe it today.

As a young guy, the Steelers games were always sold out, so I had to watch them on television. But after I got to Pitt, some of my friends and I would go to a game once in a while. What I learned from watching Terry Bradshaw was the way he threw the ball, he got rid of it quick. That was something my dad taught me, but I saw Bradshaw do it. It gave me a view of what it really takes from Bradshaw, Joe Greene, Mel Blount. I grew up watching those guys, as well as being lucky enough to throw baseball with Willie Stargell and Donn Clendenon when they lived right next to my grandmother in South Oakland.

I'm Oakland all the way through. It's always great to come home. It's emotional sometimes. Sitting on my front porch at home I could see the Cathedral of Learning. When I get out at the parking lot at Central Catholic, turn around and look over and there's the Cathedral of Learning, you remember where you grew up.

I've come a long way from Parkview Avenue now, but hard work was instilled in me at an early age. My father was a Teamster, working for the *Pittsburgh Press*. My mom worked as a school crossing guard, and I remember seeing her get dressed in winter as she was leaving to work her corner in Squirrel Hill. That's dedication to your kids, to your family, to the people in the community. That's what you do as a Pittsburgher—it's in your DNA.

I can tell you that a son couldn't ask for better parents. We were lucky to be raised in such a healthy and loving environment. My dad was my hero, my role model and the best coach I've ever had. He taught me how to believe in myself, how to throw a football, taught me about hard work, how to be positive. He always advocated for jumping rope because as a quarterback you had to be like a boxer in the ring…the core, the jumping and timing with your feet. He was ahead of his time, and it worked out okay for me. I was blessed to have him in my life.

Growing up, wanting to be a professional football player, wanting to be a quarterback—the streets of Pittsburgh, playing little league and to go into the Pro Football Hall of Fame, it's really, really special. Claire and I have appreciated the opportunity to be able to come back to the neighborhood, take our kids and grandkids and see friends, the church and the field. It brings back great memories.

Looking back on my career, I've accomplished many things. But what I cherish more than any record that I hold, any fourth-quarter comeback, any win that I was involved in, what I cherish most is the relationships that I've made, the people I've worked with, the teammates I lined up beside, the opponents that I've competed against. The friends and family—in both Pittsburgh and Miami—that's what I cherish most.

JOE NAMATH

The son of a steel worker from Beaver Falls, Joseph William Namath came from the rich football tradition that is in Pennsylvania and is best remembered for his performance in the New York Jets' stunning 16–7 upset of the heavily favored Baltimore Colts in Super Bowl III. During his thirteen-year tenure from 1965 through 1977, Namath was one of the game's most exciting, proficient and publicized quarterbacks and is regarded as one of the most important players in the NFL history. He was inducted into the Pro Football Hall of Fame in 1985. In addition to his flourishing football career, his popularity in the world of entertainment included appearances in popular films and television shows.

I believe that no matter where in the world it starts, it starts at home first if you're lucky enough to have the right guidance and love. My values and character were shaped in Beaver County, and I will be forever grateful for that. Beaver County will always hold a special place in my heart.

At home, my parents, who are of Hungarian descent, taught the children respect. I was the youngest of four boys and my sister, Rita, and we were taught respect. From there, Western Pennsylvania was wonderful. Beaver Falls, Pittsburgh, close ties, getting to see the Pirates play, that was one of the highlights of my life. The hardworking folks, my dad was a steel mill man, and it was a big day when he would take us up to the union hall and we would get a brown bag with an orange and an apple, some rock candy and I was just so damned happy. It was wonderful.

Beaver Falls had Babcock & Wilcox, Moltrup Steel and Armstrong Cork. We had the Beaver River, and it was all steel mills all the way down the valley to Pittsburgh. Our parents were hard workers. The lawyers and the doctors were the wealthiest ones, but we had humble beginnings, respecting everyone regardless of their ethnicity or color of their skin. We were a melting pot.

My family lived in a part of Beaver Falls that was called the Lower End, a low-income part of town. It was a predominately Black neighborhood, and the guys I hung out with were Black. In high school, I was the only white boy on the starting basketball team and the four other guys were Black; they were all friends of mine from the neighborhood. The only time I'd ever run into any kind of race thing had been when I was little, when me and my best friend, Linwood Alfrod, went into a pizza place and got thrown out. The lady who ran it just told us to get the hell out, so we both left.

But when I got to the University of Alabama—wow! Coming from where I came from, I couldn't believe it. Water fountains for whites were painted white; there were different bathrooms for whites and Blacks; Blacks had to sit in the backs of buses and whites had to sit up front. I just couldn't understand it.

The steel mills and the coal mines created tough, hardworking people, and the boys played football. That's what you did. When you'd go around town on a Friday night, you could break into anybody's house, but there'd be nothing to steal. I played baseball, basketball and football, and that was basically my world. My brothers Bob and Frank taught me how to play sports. The throwing motion, the attitude, the team

Courtesy Associated Press.

65

concept—that came from my brothers, but they wouldn't let me get too big of a head though.

The first quarterback that I paid a whole lot of mind to was Vito "Babe" Parilli, from Rochester, Pennsylvania, four miles down the river from Beaver Falls. Heck, when I was in the sixth grade I'd be going up to the five-and-ten at lunchtime to see my mother, who was working there. I left school to walk one block, and in that one block's walk there happened to be an Army-Navy store. And I'd stop at the store on the outside and look into the window. On the shelf there was a gold football helmet made by Hutch, and Babe Parilli had signed it.

And damned don't you know that the New York Jets traded for Babe Parilli, and in '68, in that locker room, we're sitting together side by side through training camp and everything else. And I couldn't believe I was lucky enough to be sitting beside…and having a teammate…of Babe Parilli. Boy, that was cool.

Until my senior year, baseball and basketball were my best sports. Even when I was a senior, I still wanted to play baseball professionally. Shoot, when I got those offers, I sure as hell wanted to take the money and run, but the family wanted me to go to college and I guess I agreed with them.

Football is a hard game, and you had to have perseverance. We had people like Coach Larry Bruno teaching us the values of life along with the game. Football Hall of Fame, that's wonderful, something I never dreamed about. All I ever dreamed of in sports, especially football, was winning the WPIAL championship. And we did it, and I'm a lucky guy….I get goose bumps thinking about it now!

It's true my appeal extended beyond the football field to a sense of cool. In a high school baseball team photo, I can be seen posing with sunglasses on. I think we all want to stand out. I never forgot Coach telling me to get my hair cut, and I said, "Coach, my girl wants it long." That was the truth and now, what's the big deal?

Since my parents passed away, I don't get back home as often, but whenever I do I get together with my family, old friends and teammates. It's a special feeling to be part of Beaver Falls and its sports history. I pull for these guys. The area, the love of sports and the people and the passion for all sports, especially. Pennsylvania was the third-most populated state at one time, and that's why I figured we had so many good athletes. We had more people in the state than others, but it's from your home, your background, how you're taught, your coaches, your teachers. It's the people you're around. I'm just thankful that I was able to grow up where I grew up.

I've just started the fourth quarter of my life in my opinion. I've seen many times where the game was won in the fourth quarter, and that is what I plan on doing. I recognized as I moved along in this life that I've been very lucky and fortunate. Everyone is not always dealt a full deck when they come into this world, and lady luck can be cruel. Knowing how much gratitude I should have let me put some effort into helping those that aren't so lucky.

They talk about teamwork in sports, but the biggest game of all—life—is all about teamwork....We need one another. I'm going to keep trying to make progress. I'm going to keep trying to be productive. I'm going to keep trying to enjoy life spiritually and be respectful of every single person I meet. I'm going to make this fourth quarter hopefully the best quarter I possibly can as a father, a grandfather and as a friend to everyone I'm around.

SONNY VACCARO

John Paul "Sonny" Vaccaro is an iconic sports marketing executive best known for his tenure with Nike, where he signed Michael Jordan to his first sneaker contract. He is also a former top marketer at Adidas and Reebok. He founded the ABCD All America Camp, which operated from 1984 to 2007, featuring the top high school basketball prospects in the country, and also founded, with Pat DiCesare, the Dapper Dan Roundball Classic, which was the first national high school all-star game.

The time I grew up in Trafford in 1939, it was during the war; my relatives on both sides of the family, the Mastriani and the Vaccaro familes, had a lot to do with the war effort. We lived in a very diverse community, and I was raised in the most terrible reclamation project ever after the war. I remember my nannas and my grandfathers would get together on Sundays, and we were never apart.

I lived next door to Pat DiCesare's grandmother. I have known Pat and his family all of my life, and we grew up together. I can attest that my beginnings were I grew up with family with no discretion, which was with everybody in town. We had more nationalities, more churches, than any small town in Western Pennsylvania....We were a League of Nations before anyone knew what that was.

Since I was born, I've been Pittsburgh Proud and Italian-Centric. I've been around the world, so nothing compares to my nationality and my hometown. When I say "Pittsburgh Proud," that's Pittsburgh, that whole area, because

Courtesy Ethan Miller.

everyone are different fathers and mothers and different colors, but we all seemed to get together a hell of a lot better in the worst periods of time, which were then with the war on and people not working and we overcame them. My whole existence started in Trafford with my family, my neighbors and my teammates…we grew up together and have seen the world change together.

I can't be more proud of who I am—Pittsburgh Proud and Italian-Centric—and that's because of my family and others who were part of my family growing up in the 1940s, that was the best part of my life. I started in Trafford and I'll die in Trafford, which is like saying I'll die Italian. You can change your religion and other things, but I'm Trafford and I'm Pittsburgh Proud.

There was a different animal that grew up in the steel mills, the railroads and the coal mines. I don't think there is any state in America that could have said that, and we basically started America commercially through the Carnegies, the Mellons and everybody else. Pittsburgh was once and always will because of the rivers, because of everything they had done. They were also good community people…when you look at Carnegie-Mellon University, you know who that is, how that happened. There is a history to Pittsburgh.

Before I joined Nike, the choices I made at age seventeen and when I was given a scholarship and went to Youngstown State University put me in that situation. When I went to Nike, the world changed, but the kid that went to Nike wasn't the same kid that was at Nike when we signed Michael Jordan.

When it comes to the Dapper Dan Roundball Classic, which I started with Pat, keep in mind that no one gave a shit about basketball in 1964. I had this idea when I was at Youngstown State, before the Roundball Classic, working with kids, helping to recruit players, taking them to tournaments in Sharon, Pennsylvania, and all over Pittsburgh. My life changed because I went to Pat, who was working in music, and I said to him, "I have an idea: let's bring the best basketball players in America and have them play against the best basketball players in Pennsylvania." Pat and I made it work. We went to Al Abrams at the *Pittsburgh Post-Gazette*, who guaranteed the money, before we both went off into different realms of life. I didn't have a penny, but Pat was a promoter; just like when he brought in the Beatles to Pittsburgh, Pat sold the tickets and I brought the act to him, the players, and together we created an iconic sold-out event. In 1977, we sold more tickets than Elvis Presley. We were like Martin & Lewis, a perfect team at a perfect time, the sons of Italian immigrants, who turned the town upside down with an event that had the greatest players, the tickets sold, where people still show pictures when they attended the games. We were as close as you could be, and I haven't seen him for a long time now, but we had boom-bah just by inheritance of the term.

I went to Nike in 1977, and it was a pure circumstance that I went there because of a shoe that was designed by Bobby Dieranaldo, a shoemaker in Trafford. Bobby designed the shoe, and I went out there to show them the shoe, not to work for them. My life changed in a minute, and when I was holding my basketball camps, I went to Nike to sell Bobby's shoes. Now Bobby is in the Shoemaker Hall of Fame, and while Nike didn't want Bobby's shoes, they wanted my ideas.

College basketball all changed after that, and a movie is being made, *Air: The Man Who Signed Michael Jordan.* We signed and paid the college coaches, gave them the shoes and put them on the kids. It was as simple as that, but no one ever did it. The schools bought all their shoes. Converse was the leader; Nike was a baby and did only $25 million in business the year before they met me. And that's the point: a new idea came in and it changed the basketball world.

Nike then owned the Big East. I got Nike to be the sponsor of *Big Monday Night* basketball on ESPN. I put the president of ESPN together with Phil Knight, who bought time. We had new teams and coaches: P.J. Carlesimo, Louie Carnesseca, John Thompson, Jim Calhoun…we had six Big East teams in Nike shoes, and it's the biggest show on Monday night. In 1984, Nike had all the teams in the Final Four.

My expectations were vastly, vastly exceeded with what could be done with the rights of the athlete. They have greatly exceeded them. As I associated with the lawyers and the people on the financial end, I learned. I never dreamed the kids could make zillions of dollars in one lump sum. That is the absolute truth. I couldn't have possibly thought of what was going to happen today.

But what really started it for me was when I started with Nike. When I said I would get involved was "Pay the coaches." That raised hell all over America. It did. But in reality, what I knew then—and I know it at eighty-three years old—is the athletes would get the benefit. I couldn't pay them, but I could pay them in equipment and I could pay them in the venue they're serving. They would have an opportunity to be involved. I was never a businessman, but I knew there would be nobody better than athletes to sell products. I gave the money to the coaches, but if I could have given it to the athletes in August of 1977 when I did my first deal with Nike, my God, it doesn't take a genius to understand where my mind would have been.

I don't think I've changed one bit since I was a kid in Trafford. I'm glad I ended up like I started with what my mother and dad taught me. I know that's trite, but I've never changed. I always believed in equality. I always believed the girls were just as important as the boys, that the religions had nothing to do with it and certainly the color of your skin had nothing to do with it. I've never changed. This is who I am. In Trafford, we had every nationality. We had Black families, Serbians, Polish, Italians, Irish. We had different clubs. We had like nine churches. There were only like five thousand people in the city at that time, but that whole Western Pennsylvania element was like that. We all came from the coal mines and steel mills like my dad did. He missed one day in forty-seven years. What I hope people think is I'm a pretty good guy, and I've been a pretty good guy my whole life. I've gotten in some situations I maybe shouldn't have because of political reasons or social reasons or whatever reasons. But I won't change.

I always tell my wife that when the end of my life does come and I'm gone, people will say I tried to do the right thing. I think it's very simple. I tried to do the right thing. It always didn't come out the way I tried. I didn't win every battle or argument, but I tried to do it. I hope to God I never did anything in my life that hurt anybody. If I did something, I was sincere about it, starting with the Dapper Dan. That was the wildest thing in the world to do, a basketball all-star game in Pittsburgh, Pennsylvania, where no one really cared about it. There were a few good kids, but it was all football. I think I tried. I'm happy. I feel good about my life.

ENTERTAINMENT

AHMAD JAMAL

Born Frederick Russell Jones, Ahmad Jamal is an American jazz pianist, composer, bandleader and educator. Noted for his melodic improvisations, lean style, use of space and deceptively simple embellishments, Jamal has also brought the jazz trio to the highest levels of collective expression. He is a National Endowment for the Arts (NEA) Jazz Master and won a Lifetime Achievement Grammy for his contributions to music history.

Yes, my birthplace is Pittsburgh, a town that has a lot of coal, a lot of steel mills, some great industrialists, as well as all the musicians. Pittsburgh is second to none. I came up in a high school—George Westinghouse High School—where Erroll Garner and Dodo Marmarosa also went to school, and so did Mary Lou Williams. Isn't that something? Billy Strayhorn was from my neighborhood, and there was a little tap dancer known as Gene Kelly who lived nearby, maybe you've heard of him. And then there was Mary Caldwell Dawson, my teacher who started the first African American opera company.

You see, we had an array of talent coming out of Pittsburgh, starting with Earl Hines. But don't forget about Art Blakey, and later there was George Benson, Stanley Turrentine and his brother Tommy. It goes on and on.…I can't finish the list. That's where I got all my stuff from. We also had Johnny Costa, the pianist who was on nationwide television all those years with

*Courtesy Frans
Schelleken/Redferns.*

Mister Rogers. Johnny never left Pittsburgh…what a phenomenal talent. All those masters come from Pittsburgh.

I grew up orchestrally in Pittsburgh, playing professionally in union halls and nightclubs. I'd do algebra during intermission, between sets. I was playing with Honey Boy Minor and guys sixty years old when I was eleven because I knew the repertoire. We had the musicians union. The union had a sixteen-year-old minimum age, and I joined the union when I was fourteen. I escalated my age, and the president was from Homewood, so he knew I wasn't sixteen.

I played with many, many orchestras, so I always maintained an orchestra in my head. That's why I don't like to refer to my group as a trio. I prefer to call it an ensemble because I've played with ensembles all my life. At Westinghouse High, I played in the junior orchestra and the senior orchestra, and our music director, Carl McVicker, started something called the K-Dets, which was very innovative. It was an all-American orchestra, playing both European classical music and American classical music, jazz, in the 1940s.

What I really like to remember about coming up in Pittsburgh is the fact that we didn't have this terrible separation between the classicists and contemporary musicians, jazz musicians. You had to study Beethoven and Bach, Duke Ellington and Art Tatum. You had to study both worlds, the European classical music as well as the American classical music, which some people call jazz. I rather hate the word, but for want of a replacement at this time, I'll say there weren't any lines of demarcation separating classical and jazz—we studied everything. Which is what Duke Ellington subscribed to… what he used to say is "music is of two kinds—good or bad."

I remember vividly as a child playing both Franz Liszt and Ellington in competition. Then there were the great jam sessions we had 'til four, five in the morning, which were historic and certainly priceless as far as education for the young musician was concerned. It's something that is not happening today, there or anywhere. That's how I met Art Tatum, in a jam session.

My aunt, who was an educator in North Carolina, sent me many, many compositions via sheet music, and that's how I gained the vast repertoire that you hear me indulge in. I was sent those things by her gracious efforts from ten years old and on. So my Aunt Louise was the one responsible for me acquiring that vast repertoire of standards.

People have described in many various ways my music. They call it silence, space, economy, blah, blah, blah. I call it discipline. In order to do anything successful, you have to observe certain disciplines. I don't care if it's sports, medicine or driving a car, you have to stop. You have to observe the stop signs.

The fact is that all Pittsburghers are uniquely different. No one plays piano like Erroll Garner. No one plays bass like Ray Brown. No one plays piano like Earl Hines. No one plays drums like Art Blakey. No one plays saxophone like Stanley Turrentine. We all have ushered in a different era that's just one of the unique phenomena of Pittsburgh. No one danced like Gene Kelly. No one interpreted Liszt quite like Earl Wild. Lorin Maazel, the conductor, is from Pittsburgh too. Andy Warhol is from Pittsburgh. It goes on and on. It's very difficult for me to exhaust the list, but all of us are different and unique so it's just a phenomenon that all of us have a different approach. This is a thing that happened to me as a result of growing up there, I followed that same pattern.

It's not like other cities. Pittsburgh is phenomenal. That's the difference.

ANTOINE FUQUA

Antoine Fuqua is an American filmmaker, known for his work in the action and thriller genres. He was originally known as a director of music videos and made his film debut in 1998 with The Replacement Killers. *His critical breakthrough was the award-winning 2001 crime thriller* Training Day.

I was born in the Hill District and grew up in Homewood, and my childhood helped shape my worldview as a man and it still affects how I make movies.

Courtesy Frederic Kern/
Geisler-Fotopress.

I had a great family, beautiful mother, father, cousins and all that stuff. The violence that took place around us was part of the world that we unfortunately all lived in because of economics. What affected me most was that Pittsburgh is a tough town. Got to play football, basketball, baseball. It's cold in the winter. It's like *Deer Hunter.*

It's a place where the cliché is: men are men. When you grow up and have kids, what does that really mean? It can get you in trouble because you don't ask for help as you should. I've carried that with me. I've seen friends and family members that way. I try to put some of that in the movies. I had a very spiritual youth. I went to church every day. So that's in all my movies as well.

Pittsburgh is a big influence on my way of thinking. The town's changing, and so is the idea of masculinity. I love my friends and family in Pittsburgh. They're beautiful people, and I wouldn't be here without them.

Sports has always been a big part of bringing people together. I played baseball, football and basketball, and my cousin Frenchy was the intended target on Franco Harris's Immaculate Reception. I remember the celebrations when (the Pirates won) and feeling like I was part of a bigger thing. I wasn't just a Black kid living in Homewood. We were all Pirates fans. We were all from Pittsburgh. It was like we were all a part of it. And the fact they were of color made us more connected.

When I was younger, growing up in Pittsburgh, a professor suggested that I take an art class, and the art class I fell in love with and the idea of being an artist. I fell in love with an artist by the name of Caravaggio, a baroque painter, on the streets of Italy. A bit of a troublemaker, he actually got in a duel over a woman and killed a guy; eventually he was hunted down and killed. But he was an amazing artist, and there was a big lesson in that for me: that artists don't always come from money.

In the same art class, I discovered Akira Kurosawa, who was a painter, and his storyboards were a subject of conversation one day. He did the film *Seven Samurai*, and I watched the *Magnificent Seven*, and those movies are influential when you're a kid because I loved westerns. It was something that happened inside of me, an awakening of a part of me that I didn't know existed. I didn't realize that I had a passion to tell stories until then. Kurosawa remains the most guiding influence in my life. It's not necessarily what you would expect from a kid who grew up in the Pittsburgh ghetto.

It's interesting, Pittsburgh has always been leading the charge for some reason. I think it's because it's a pretty diverse city. People may not realize that, but it is. To take a team all Latino or Black and put them on the field, you're taking a risk right there. They could have riots break out. God knows what can happen. But the appreciation and love of the game and the fact they played well and were winning, that kind of changes everything. Somehow if you win, people forget all of the other silliness. It's amazing.

It's an easy city to live in. It's close to New York, close to Philly. It's one of these cities that is not too big. And I think sports has always been leading the charge with segregation. It's always been a place that, since it's a sports climate, it's always sort of brought different races together for a winning goal.

The first films of my career were music videos, and I still feel that combining film and music are a deep part of who I am. I was taking an art class and studying different time periods and movements, and one day we were doing Asian art and a still came up from *Ran*. Storyboards were paintings, and I remembered seeing those images before. I loved movies. I loved watching westerns with my grandmother, who knew every action film, and loved westerns because she was southern.

I loved sneaking into the second feature in some theaters downtown. That was my escape. I'd go to the Regency Theatre and watch obscure karate films and Bruce Lee. And one day they happened to have a Japanese bill, and it just blew me away. I didn't even know what a samurai was. But I was completely transported. I'm a product of older filmmakers, I guess, the past where you get to make movies and scenes are what they are.

I watched the *Seven Samurai* a lot because I loved it growing up. I can't describe to you how powerful that was. When you're a kid, you can't watch an almost-three-hour movie, but this was a war I just never saw before, with these samurai. I could relate to it, just being poor.

Forever Brothers, a documentary about the 1971 World Series–winning Pittsburgh Pirates squad that fielded the first entirely Black and Latino lineup in major-league history, has to do with Pittsburgh. It has to do with diversity, which is obviously important to me and the world today, and especially to sports, as well. How people come together, sometimes taking a risk.

Perseverance, being brave, stepping into the world. The biggest thing is my grandmother prayed all day from before the sun came up—it was all about God and family. Definitely family, doing whatever it takes to get back to family, so that all goes back to Pittsburgh.

BILLY GARDELL

Billy Gardell took the long road to Hollywood, stopping at every small-town lounge, military base and comedy club along the way. His comedy act took him to Los Angeles, where his dedication to acting, along with touring as a stand-up comedian, allowed him to grow consistently in both arenas. Gardell is best known to television audiences for his portrayal of one of the title characters on the sitcoms Mike & Molly *and* Bob Hearts Abishola.

I come from Pittsburgh, which is a steel town, a hardworking town. They have this habit of, "Let's make light of it so we can get through a tough situation." So that's kind of where my humor comes from.

I was a real Pittsburgh kid. Alleys were my playgrounds, and we played ball on fields that weren't in great shape. Before laptops and apps, I caught lightning bugs, played hide-and-seek and sat under trees with my buddies figuring out what we were going to do that day. My generation is the last bus from the old school before they closed it up. I cherish that.

I was one of those kids who didn't quite fit in. I was skipping school. I got into a little mischief, but nothing too bad. This is what I was doing when I was nine on Harrison Avenue. There used to be a '70s show called *SWAT*. Me and three of my buddies, my porch was headquarters and we had sticks for guns and we had a mission. That's all I'm doing.

My work ethic and humor come from Pittsburgh. I have uncles and aunts, dear friends, my cousin's a cop there, my uncle worked for U.S. Steel, my grandfather worked for the Switch and Signal Railroad, my mother never had less than two jobs and my father, Bill, painted houses and then worked in a bank. A lot of working-class pride comes out of that place. When our town unifies, it just becomes the Terrible Towel.

What I noticed about my relatives, and my dad's buddies, is how they got through their days by making light of their situation. Humor does that, especially in adverse times. And my dad took great pride in being a Pittsburgher. It gets me a little emotional. This city is who I am.

Courtesy Michael Yarish/CBS Entertainment.

I haven't lived there for over twenty-five years, but Pittsburgh is in my heart. I tell my son, Will, when you walk out that door, it's Los Angeles out there. But when you come in here and shut that door, it's Pittsburgh in here. And oh yeah, he's being made into a Steelers fan; he doesn't have a choice.

When it comes to Pittsburgh's professional sports teams, you'll often find me at Pirates games when I'm home. I'm a die-hard. I watch them and they torture me. The Steelers have been very kind to me. I've been on the sideline and do the Terrible Towel twirl, and because of that I struck up a friendship with Franco [Harris], been with Ben [Roethlisberger], Rocky [Bleier], Mel [Blount], [Jerome] Bettis. So for a kid from Harrison Avenue to walk down on that sideline, that's a dream. I really don't know how I can top that.

I hold on to Pittsburgh in everything I do. Cheeseburgers are my downfall. Well, cheeseburgers and coming home to Pittsburgh. I got to hit Primanti's, Veltre's for pizza. My wife knows if I come to Pittsburgh, all bets are off for a couple of days.

Joe O'Connell, my best friend, and I met in the early '90s when Joe worked in the kitchen of the Funny Bone in Monroeville, where I performed stand-up comedy. He was the kitchen manager, and we just hit it off and became super-fast friends. A bond formed, and about three years later we decided to move to California together and come out here and chase this fantasy. Then we try to find other Pittsburghers.

You know it's just different, it's a different kind of sarcasm. Pittsburgh has a wonderful way of work ethic, family and don't take yourself too seriously. And L.A., it's a place where people are trying to break into the business, and it doesn't have the feel Pittsburgh has for me and that's okay. That's who I am out there. L.A. is a very transient place—everybody's from someplace else in most of the city. So I just hold on to what I learned and who I am in the way of Pittsburgh.

BILLY HARTUNG

Actor, singer, dancer and educator Billy Hartung has more than one thousand performances on the Broadway stage to his credit. He has been featured in three Broadway shows: Side Show, Footloose *and* Minnelli on Minnelli. *He can also be seen singing and dancing in the Academy Award–winning movie musical* Chicago. *Hartung is currently the executive director of the Center for Theater Arts, which offers an award-winning professional curriculum of more than eighty classes in the performing arts. He is the father of six children.*

I'm one of seven children, the middle child of two blue-collar parents who worked to raise their family that would all have different dreams. I'm an artist, but I have a brother who is a police officer, sisters who are teachers, a brother that is a contractor, so we all had aspirations for careers. My dad was an only child who now had seven kids in a house bustling like crazy, where we grew up simple but we were able to dream big.

One of the reasons I moved forward with my arts and performing career, it really wasn't about the show, it was just about me being a kid. I was doing a Broadway show, and I said to my brother Dan, "Hey are you coming up to see the show?" and he said, "Bill, do you watch me work?" And he didn't mean anything by it except he was proud of me, and that's the path I chose. As kids growing up in Pittsburgh, we all had different needs, and my parents made sure that happened.

I went through Mount Lebanon school system, but then I transferred to Seton LaSalle because Mount Lebanon was way too big for me. Seton was much smaller, and it gave me a place for me to harness my love of theater. And I went to the Center for Theater Arts, which I now run, so my bubble just keeps getting more beautiful.

It wasn't that I wanted to be in musical theater; it was the movie *Grease*. I was in second grade: I liked the hair and the random outbreak of song over and over, and I thought that whole Danny Zuko thing is pretty cool. We had a block party in our neighborhood, and the kids would do a variety show every year and we decided to put on the movie *Grease*. I was Danny in the second grade, and a twelfth grader on my street was Sandy, and I was like I love this singing and dancing thing.

I found a joy in performing, and it was a bunch of guys running around with their cars and leather jackets and it ended up being a version of *Footloose* for me which was all great fun. I had the Center for Theater Arts, which, in fourth grade, was the first school where I took an acting class. And they said,

"Hey, do you want to be in shows? Take dance classes." That's really how I got my start. It was the better part of ten years, and I did everything that I could during that time.

As I got older and at Point Park, I loved making people's dreams come true. When people said I'm working on a new show and how do you string a story along, I loved being wacky. And I thought, "If this is what it's about, I like making people happy and creating things."

Courtesy Center for Theater Arts.

Don Brockett was the first person to employ me as a professional, and he created a window for me. And then Danny Herman came into town, and he was a major influencer and mentor because he was also a very energetic, committed dancer who had already been performing on Broadway.

To reflect on growing up here, I knew when I was in New York, I was looking for a place like Pittsburgh in Connecticut, New Jersey or Queens, but I couldn't find it. Now, I found really good people and really wonderful communities, but I didn't envision growing my family in a town like that, whereas I watched my family grow in a town like Pittsburgh and saw it work.

My dream was to have this big, beautiful family that I have. How I was going to take care of them was the recipe for success in whatever I did, but I knew I could do it here because I watched my family thrive. Now my kids are around like twenty-some cousins, everyone is within eight miles of each other. Family means a lot, and this is a town where that's a currency.

When my parents would drive Billy Porter back into the city on Tuesday nights after class at CTA, there wasn't anything to gain from it except helping someone find their way. What it did do was set an example that you can always find the time to help someone find their way. We always had five other kids at our house for dinner…my parents never just fed seven kids, they fed twelve to twenty constantly. There's a goodness in that and says a lot about meeting people where they are, which is just so Pittsburgh.

People in New York would say to me, "What the hell are you doing here? You got it all in Pittsburgh." And when you're in Pittsburgh people think, "Don't you want to go out there and do something?" I never say I came back, I say I came forward to something I knew was worth reaching for, which was a place to set your roots and grow.

I don't think talent has a zip code, and that's why there's so much success here. I did the Academy Awards and the Kennedy Center Honors when I lived in Pittsburgh. I was called to do a number of readings and workshops; nobody cared what my zip code was, they just wanted to know if I could make it.

Work ethic, sweat equity and emotional currency is big, so all of those have value in Pittsburgh regardless of what career you take; you eventually climb the ladder of perceived success. What people find out from Pittsburgh is that hard work, that work ethic, that determination, that commitment, that's all they know.

When you meet people who have done well who are from Pittsburgh and you come in the room, Rob Marshall knew I was from Pittsburgh. He watched me on crew in a show, and when I showed up he was like, "Yep, there you are, I knew it was only a matter of time before you would show up here." There's no BS meter. It is what it is and it's authentic.

BILLY PORTER

William Ellis Porter II is an American actor, singer, writer and director. He graduated from Carnegie Mellon University School of Drama, and he achieved fame performing on Broadway before starting a solo career as a singer and actor. He won the 2013 Tony Award for Best Actor in a Musical and a Grammy for his portrayal of drag performer Lola in Kinky Boots.

The curtain went up late on the first performance of *Kinky Boots* because it's uncommon these days to have the 2,800-seat Benedum Center sold out. I hadn't had a chance to breathe since my feet hit the pavement in Pittsburgh. It was better that way. No time to stress out. No time for fear to creep in.

This prodigal son hath come home—*as a lady*! Theater cracked open a space for me to dream beyond my circumstance.

The spotlight blinds me. All I see is void. Black. The crowd erupts as if I were Beyoncé. My breath is taken away by the sheer force of the love I feel. Is this love true? Accepting? Unconditional? Can I trust this uncomplicated support I feel, when not so long ago the very archetype I represent was vilified and reviled?

Being Black, gay and Christian in Pittsburgh during the 1980s made me a target for the kind of oppression that literally kills people and destroys humanity. Government- and religion-sanctioned homophobia permeated the culture here.

From the moment I could comprehend thoughts and ideas, the well-intentioned adults closest to me—loved ones, preachers and educators—took turns trying to silence me. Sometimes unconsciously or so I tell myself. Always aggressively. *Abomination* was the word most used to describe me in the structure of my family and religion. *Faggot* was the term of choice in most other circles.

Then there was the time a family friend threatened me with death if I ever turned gay. Or the time I was fag-bashed only a couple doors down from the stage door of the Benedum Center as I headed into Pegasus, a downtown gay bar.

You see, I represented something that made people feel uncomfortable. My ministry and very presence awakened something in people around me that begged [for] a conversation nobody was ready to have. The only way I knew to save myself was to get out of Pittsburgh until they could. So I did. And I didn't come home for decades. I put blinders on and simply put one foot in front of the other—staving off, as best I could, all negativity in my path.

It's fascinating to me that sometimes, when one is in the trenches, focused and fighting for so long, the very fruits of that labor often go unseen because the fight becomes the normal. I am amazed now that Pittsburgh has shown me that we live in a time of a "new normal."

Courtesy Shavonne Wong.

When Ms. Lola's anthem "Hold Me in Your Heart" received that five-minute standing ovation on opening night, I felt my blinders melt away. I felt my own heart—which I had kept closed and guarded for so many years—crack open. For the first time in decades, my eyes were opened to the evolution and transformation that the people of Pittsburgh have been engaged in.

I see my old neighborhood of East Liberty emerging as a cultural leader as well as a melting pot of cross-cultural opportunity. Downtown is percolating with the kind of diversity that attracts more than 2 million people each year to its epicenter in the Cultural District. The

81

explosion of the arts in every nook and cranny of the city astounds me—from South Side's City Theatre to North Side's Mattress Factory. There's music and dance and theater and visual stimulation surrounding all of our three rivers, and I am so honored to call Pittsburgh my home.

While I have been living in my adopted home of New York City for the past thirty-five years, I know I would not be the person I am today if not for my time in da 'Burgh, and I look forward to being a fully engaged participant in all that is Pittsburgh culture for the rest of my days.

Who knew? With one strike of my stacked stiletto, *Kinky Boots* helped crack open an inspiring conversation and pierce an archaic collective fear as society moves closer to accepting people for who they are more than I ever could have dreamed. I'm so grateful to have fought hard enough and lived long enough to see this essential growth. And now I'm ready to receive the love without suspicion. I am ready to honor the journey. For the journey is the gift. One can't have a testimony without a test.

Therefore, I now must choose joy. I must choose love. I must choose forgiveness.

I thank those angels who showed up for me at every fork and block in the road—whose support and unconditional love lifted me up and kept me sane. On paper, I was dismissed as a probable statistic. But God had a different plan.

Thank you, Pittsburgh, for your gifts of growth, evolution and acceptance. It's so good to have a place I can truly call home. You are all proof that you change the world when you change your mind!

BURTON MORRIS

Internationally recognized pop artist Burton Morris is best known for his bold and graphic depictions of American icons and brands. His subject matter includes objects that portray today's popular culture. His distinctive art style is characterized by radiant black outlines and vivid colors that emit energy in all of his work and put an energetic and colorful spin on today's culture.

Growing up in Pittsburgh during the 1960s, I had an early attraction to art. My parents used to take me to the Carnegie Museum, which was minutes from where we lived in Squirrel Hill. I loved being surrounded by all of the amazing artwork and historic artifacts that were there.

When I was three and a half years old, I was swinging on monkey bars pretending to be Tarzan of the apes and jumped off the bars and fell to the ground, breaking my left femur bone. At that time in 1967, when you broke your femur bone, you were confined to a full-body cast for two months. All I was able to do was move my upper torso and arms. My parents gave me crayons, pencils and paper to draw on, and this is when my love for drawing started.

I was always fascinated with comic books and drawing superheroes. I was enamored with the primary colors and line art of each comic book panel and would spend hours daily drawing my own comic book artworks. I experimented with all types of art materials and loved working in pen and ink. I once drew a portrait of Stan Lee when I was ten years old and later gave it to him as a thank-you for being such a huge inspiration to me. Years later, Stan asked me to create a depiction of the Silver Surfer, which hung behind his desk for years in his office.

Around the age of twelve, I discovered the work of Albrecht Durer, a sixteenth-century artist who was known for his meticulous engravings. I would emulate his style of engraving in all of my art with pen and ink. This technique has helped to define my art style that I am known for today.

Throughout my school years, I developed a reputation of being known as the artist of the class. In 1986, I earned my Bachelor of Fine Arts degree at Carnegie Mellon University.

After a brief stint working as an art director directing television commercials in advertising in Pittsburgh, I struck out on my own, establishing the Burton Morris Studios in 1990. That year I began making my small, pop iconic drawings into large-scale paintings. I chose one subject per composition to create "an instant happening" for the viewer.

My first big break that exposed my art to the world came in 1993, when Absolut Vodka selected my artwork to represent Pennsylvania for its Absolut Statehood campaign. Pop Art legend Andy Warhol, who opened up the doors for what I do today, had created the first Absolut advertisement. It was very prestigious as an artist to be a part of this amazing campaign, and it was my first national exposure of my artwork debuting in both *TIME* magazine and *USA Today*.

In 1994, my artwork began to hang in Central Perk, the fictitious coffee shop on the hit NBC sitcom *Friends*. Starting with the third episode, David Schwimmer wore a T-shirt of mine of a baseball player in the scene. It was a very lucky break, as I had started a T-shirt company, and apparently one of the cameramen for the show gave it to him to wear on set.

Above and opposite: Courtesy Burton Morris Studios.

After the episode aired, I contacted Kevin Bright, the creator of the show, and met with him to choose new paintings to display on future shows. He introduced me to the cast members early on, and I'll never forget wishing all of them good luck on their new TV show! Over the years, the show featured over a dozen original paintings of mine in Central Perk Coffee Shop, such as the steaming *Coffee Cup*, *Statue of Liberty*, *King Kong* and *Uncle Sam* to name a few. All in all, my paintings were seen in over seventy-five episodes throughout the course of *Friends'* ten seasons. The

success of the show becoming a global pop phenomenon helped to establish my style and artwork in today's pop culture.

Since then, I have showcased my original artworks in galleries and exhibitions worldwide. My artwork has been selected as the signature image for the FIFA World Cup Soccer Games, the 76th Annual Academy Awards, the 38th Montreux Jazz Festival, the 2004 Summer Olympic Games and the 2006 MLB All-Star Game.

Collectors of my art range from Brad Pitt, Oprah Winfrey, Ralph Lauren, President Barack Obama and Tommy Hilfiger to Stan Lee, Andre Agassi and Fred Rogers.

Original artworks have been commissioned for corporations and institutions such as Perrier, H.J. Heinz, Chanel, AT&T, Kellogg's, Rolex and the U.S. State Department. My artwork is featured in the collections of the United Nations, the Albright-Knox Museum, the Jimmy Carter Center, the Elysee Museum, the World of Coca-Cola Museum and the Academy of Motion Picture Arts & Sciences.

In addition, my artwork has helped to raise millions of dollars globally for countless charities over the years.

I am so fortunate to be surrounded by my beautiful wife, Sara, and my three incredible daughters here in Los Angeles. I'm always trying to reinvent myself, always thinking about creating new ideas for the future. While my dad always asked if I could make a living doing this, my parents always instilled the belief that if you believe in yourself, you could do anything. It's interesting the journey it's taken me, and the amazing people I've met.

CHRIS FRANTZ

Charton Christopher Frantz is an American musician and record producer. He is the drummer for both the Talking Heads and Tom Tom Club, both of which he co-founded with wife and Talking Heads bassist Tina Weymouth. In 2002, Frantz was inducted into the Rock & Roll Hall of Fame as a member of Talking Heads.

My father was from Pittsburgh and was in the military, and the military sent him to Harvard Law School and he became an army lawyer in the Judge Advocate General or JAG school, which is different than what it means in Pittsburgh. He decided that after teaching at the JAG school he would go into private practice, and his contacts were in Pittsburgh because he grew up in Pittsburgh between East Liberty and Oakland. He moved the family back to Pittsburgh and became a junior partner at Buchanan Ingersoll. Our first home was in the north hills, and I went to Berkeley Hills Elementary School. And it was at that school one day that my class was taken to the gymnasium, and we were given a musical instrument called the flutophone and they taught us to play very basic songs like "Mary Had a Little Lamb." I would have been in the second grade, and I really liked it. I wasn't crazy about the flutophone itself, but I really liked playing music and I had always enjoyed listening to my parents' great collection of calypso records.

Eventually, my parents decided our apartment was too small and decided to move to O'Hara Township when I was in fourth grade. By that time, I was playing the trumpet, but it really wasn't working out for me. I had a very perceptive music teacher at Kerr School, Gene Wilmouth, and I explained my problem. He said, "Well, Chris, you have a good sense of rhythm. What do you think if we switch you over to the drums?" He was a percussionist himself, a mallet instrument guy, xylophone, piano and drums. He gave me the little rubber practice pad, a pair of sticks and a book of rudiments, and every week I would get a lesson from him. After about a year's time, I was doing really well on the drums and I was able to be a member of the school band....I just loved it, and it was my favorite activity at school. After Kerr

Courtesy Jim Dyson/Getty.

School, I went to Aspinwall Junior High, and I had another band teacher there, Charles Springman. And it was there that I met Lloyd Stamy. Lloyd played trumpet, and I was playing drums. Mr. Springman was very serious, a real tough guy but a sweetheart underneath all that, and he was like, "If you don't keep up with your band lessons and can't hang with the rest of the band, you're out." That was his introduction to junior high band the first day of school.

One night, America was watching *The Ed Sullivan Show* and the Beatles came on. That changed everything, kind of overnight, so together with Lloyd, Ernie Meynard who played trombone, Ray Bayer who played the clarinet but in our band he played lead guitar, Tom Kleeb who played rhythm guitar and Herb Purcell on bass, we started a band, the Lost Chords.

I went away to boarding school for two years and came back to Pittsburgh and enrolled in Shadyside Academy. I had friends that were in bands and rock-and-roll bands particularly, and I would watch them rehearse and found it very exciting. I thought, "Oh, their drummer is so good I could never hope to replace him or I could never hope to be in a band anymore."…I thought I wasn't good enough. But I kept my drums in my basement, and I would play along with records, put on headphones and bash away. Songs that I would play along with at that time were the Rolling Stones and I really liked soul music so James Brown, Wilson Pickett, Sam & Dave, Booker T. & the M.G.'s, Motown, too, but I particularly loved the southern soul music.

Then I got serious about art at Shadyside Academy, where I had a really great art teacher named David Miller, who introduced me to the whole contemporary art scene, which I knew nothing about. I'm talking about Andy Warhol, Willem de Kooning, Jackson Pollock and Robert Rauschenberg. I got really into it; drawing and painting kind of replaced music for me for a while. I was still practicing drums in my basement, but I wasn't active in a band. I got better and better at painting, and one day Mr. Miller said to me, "Chris, I think you should go to the Rhode Island School of Design." So I applied, got in and it was there that I met Tina Weymouth (who became my wife), David Byrne and some other guys. Tina wasn't in our first band called the Artistics. It was a cover band for the most part, but David and I said to each other, "We should try writing songs of our own." It was there that we wrote "Psycho Killer," which was on the first Talking Heads album and always a real crowd pleaser.

Visual art, painting and drawing, kind of go hand in hand. It's really the same artistic impulse that makes you want to write a song or play the drums or the guitar. I felt like I had the best of both worlds…at RISD I could do painting and I could also be in a rock band. After we graduated from RISD, David and I along with Tina decided we would move to New York City. I was trying to get Tina to join the band all this time, but she just refused. She was like, "No, no, I love your band but this is not for me. That's guy stuff." Rock-and-roll is a boys club, and I think she foresaw a lot of trouble. Tina was determined to become a painter and David and I were determined to start a rock band, and we started practicing together.

Tina, David and I lived all together in the same loft on the Lower East Side of New York, a bad neighborhood. Just one block off the Bowery, but we found this place called CBGB's, which was where very interesting bands played original material. The first bands we saw there was the Ramones, then Patti Smith and a band called Television, so it confirmed to me that CBGB's was a very influential place, kind of like the way the Cavern Club in Liverpool had been for the Beatles and all of those Merseybeat bands. Our band then played there; the audience was very sparse in the early days of CBGB's…there would be ten maybe twenty people in the audience, but as things developed and as our band got better sooner than later there were lines around the block.

It was a very exciting time for us. I would continue to go back to Pittsburgh to visit my parents, and I remained friends with many of the people I went to school with at Shadyside Academy and Aspinwall Junior High School. I was fortunate to have some very good teachers and was always grateful because they steered me in the right direction. I wanted to be an artist, but it didn't matter to me whether it was painting or music—I just wanted to satisfy myself for self-expression. My teachers encouraged and nourished that for me, and my parents were very good at supporting those dreams. And years later, the band we started at CBGB's in New York became Talking Heads.

I was looking recently at a photo that was posted on Facebook which was the first article that was written about the Talking Heads in the *New York Times*, April 1976. We had not even made a record deal yet, but we were in the *New York Times*. We got to perform on *American Bandstand* in 1978, and that was a big deal for us. Dick Clark was really on top of his game, sat down with us before the show, wanted to make sure that all of the information that was given to him about us was correct. And he was just a really good guy in a very empathetic way, which I appreciated.

One thing I always loved about Pittsburgh was going to the Pittsburgh Symphony. It wasn't rock-and-roll, but it was very impressive music. And I was very moved by it. And they would perform at the Syria Mosque back in those days, and I just loved it. I truly enjoyed the Carnegie Museums, both the art museum and the natural history museum. I would ride my bicycle there across the Highland Park Bridge and into Oakland, lock up my bike and eat in the cafeteria downstairs. I just loved that and would wander around.

In my high school years, there was something also at Carnegie Library called the International Poetry Forum, directed by Ted Hazlett and Sam Hazo. I went to that religiously. I was very interested in poetry, and I met the great poet Robert Lowell, who happened to be in Pittsburgh the same day that his picture appeared on the cover of *TIME* magazine, and I got his autograph. At the International Poetry Forum, they would also have people like Judy Collins who would perform. It was cultural things like that and just knowing that Andy Warhol grew up on the hillside overlooking the steel mills in Oakland. These are things that made me aware that while I enjoyed my life in Pittsburgh, it made me understand that there was a much bigger world out there and that I felt that I could be part of that—that anything was possible if you put your mind to it.

Now we're in the Rock & Roll Hall of Fame, for the past twenty years, we recently got a lifetime achievement Grammy Award, our movie *Stop Making Sense* is in the national film archive, our album *Remain in Light* is in the National Recording Archive, so I feel like it really doesn't get any better than that when it comes to awards. I took full advantage of the cultural amenities in Pittsburgh and ended up okay.

DONNIE IRIS

Born Dominic Ierace, Donnie Iris is an American rock musician known for his work with the Jaggerz and Wild Cherry during the 1970s and for his solo career beginning in the 1980s with his band the Cruisers.

Ellwood City was a great place to grow up, Crescent Avenue near Tenth Street. It was a mill town. My dad worked in the steel mill just like basically everybody else did. We had a great childhood thanks to my family. My father and mother also were raised in Ellwood City, and I had a sister, Caren. We always had a dog and frequently visited Cascade Park in New Castle and Idora Park in Youngstown.

I used to get out of bed in the morning and walk across the street to West End School. My song "10th Street" is about the school and the kids I grew up with and, later on, the bars we hung out in.

The entire neighborhood, we would get together to play baseball or basketball or football; we always found something to do. In the backyard, we produced plays and musicals with performances by the Donnie Iris Dancers. For a stage curtain, we'd have a bedspread on the line in the backyard. And all the neighborhood moms would sit on chairs, and we'd sing and dance and put on plays.

Courtesy Talent Network.

I loved baseball, but my mother had an old upright piano in their basement and taught me how to sing. She was the one who influenced me and made me sit down and sing rather than going out and playing baseball. She would insist I come in and sing. At the time, I really wasn't crazy about doing it, especially when my voice was changing, but I'm certainly glad I did it now.

At the age of five, I was singing for folks at weddings. It went from the Las Vegas kind of thing to people rocking out with Chuck Berry. I remember seeing him on TV, you know, *The Ed Sullivan Show*. I remember seeing Elvis, the Beatles, stuff like that, and they were young kids and I figured, yeah, this is more me than Sinatra and those guys.

My greatest memories of radio are from high school, listening to the powerful AM stations like WLS out of Chicago and WABC out of New York and listening to what was popular at the time. I can remember driving around in my car, me and my buddy, just enjoying what was out there. One song I remember in particular was "A Hundred Pounds of Clay" by Gene McDaniels in the early '60s. That really stuck with me.

Learning songs like that and listening to music was fine with me in high school, but I put the guitar down before I went to college. As a kid, everybody wanted to be a baseball player or a football player, but when I knew I was way too small for any of that stuff, I decided early on, "Okay, well, I'll just go to college and maybe be a teacher or something like that."

Well, when that happened, I knew it wasn't for me. I started practicing more and decided to leave Slippery Rock after about two and a half years, and that's when we founded the Jaggerz. That would have been around 1964.

When I dropped out of college to pursue music, I wasn't worried about my mom's reaction, but I thought my dad was going to kill me! Quite the contrary, he wished me well and said, "Go for it!" That really gave me the confidence I needed. When they saw the successes, they, of course, were elated and very proud.

There were times when I thought about moving away, to New York City or Los Angeles or Nashville, to be closer to the music industry. But I never felt tempted by the bright lights of celebrity. I would have never felt comfortable doing that. I felt if I could do something, I could do it right here.

I was on *American Bandstand*, but that was years earlier with the Jaggerz. "The Rapper" is the biggest record I ever had. It's one of those things that just happened. You go in the studio and record something, then you hear it on the radio and think, "Holy crap, what's going on?"

When our popular song "Ah! Leah!" broke, it was crazy because nobody expected anything. Mark Avsec and I just went into the studio to do some recordings. We didn't even have a band at the time; we just hired these guys to come into the studio and play. We ended up getting all this airplay, and we pretty much had to put a band together. I went to all the guys who played on the sessions and said, "Do you want to go out on the road and promote this?" and everybody was into it. We rehearsed a couple of weeks, and off we went.

As far as airplay, "Ah! Leah!" was being played all over the country. We were able to tour everywhere. But nowhere else was it like Cleveland or Pittsburgh. Those cities embraced us like crazy.

Oh man, it's great. People keep coming to see us, and we enjoy getting together after all these years. We're doing maybe ten to twelve shows a year at the most, so it's not like we're getting burned out or anything. We try to put the beauty with the beast. That's what we've always called most of our music. We love the way rock music pounds and kicks, but we also love melodies and harmonies. We try to mix it all together.

At a certain point, I became a meme for the former morning team at WDVE Radio, Scott Paulsen and Jim Krenn. I think something happened, somebody called in and said they saw me pumping gas at the gas station or something, and they just rolled with it, man. They started making stuff up, and then other people called in that they would see me here or there and it just snowballed. I made fun of myself, they made fun of me and, you know, I gave it right back to them.

It was huge, it was a huge impact. They kind of brought it to iconic effing measures. They were on it all the time. People would see me at gas stations or in Giant Eagle, and they would make up these skits like I was working at Pants 'n At with my brother Ronnie. They were hilarious, and that helped to keep it going, because, for a while there, we weren't recording or doing anything. You know, we had our ups and downs, but they kept it going.

I live not far from downtown Pittsburgh now in Coraopolis. I don't like winter, but other than that, being around Pittsburgh is great. I have friends and family here; that's really why I've stayed. I can't see myself moving away.

I wouldn't change anything about growing up in Western Pennsylvania. It's got everything. Besides being a great small town, I guess you'd call it, it's got the sports that everybody likes, it's got culture, it's got the museums, anything.

Everything you'd want is right here, and the people, they're Yinzers. They're just a great, great bunch of people. It's just a great place to live.

ED DRISCOLL

Ed Driscoll is an Emmy Award–winning comedian, writer, producer and speaker. A bright and clever stand-up comic, he has showcased his quick wit on television programs from Politically Incorrect *to NBC's* Comedy Showcase. *Driscoll has written for various television series such as* The Drew Carey Show *and* Dennis Miller Live, *television specials including the Academy Awards and Comic Relief and various feature films such as* Scooby Doo *and* National Security.

I knew really early, fifth grade for sure, I had a natural thing for making people laugh and would say I'm going to go in here and make people laugh today. I started listening to Robert Klein albums, particularly *Child of the 50s*, which I consider the funniest album ever made. He was my guy, and I loved listening to his stuff. Klein came to Pittsburgh to open for Helen Reddy at the Syria Mosque, and my sister and I went to the show. Klein was great as I expected, but sadly, most of the crowd was there to hear Helen roar… in numbers too big to ignore. I got a lot of puzzled looks from people as I stood and clapped and laughed and hollered during his performance. Little could I have known that ten years later, I myself would be the opening act for Robert Klein when he played Pittsburgh.

But back in 1975, inspired by Klein's work, I entered an eighth-grade talent show. I knocked 'em dead with an impression of our gym teacher, Mr. Schwartz, perfectly mimicking his staccato speech patterns and quirky physical movements. I always regret that he's not more well known because that's the impression I do best, but no one knows it beyond Our Lady of Grace School.

It was then that I realized I might actually have a future with what eventually would become my true love of comedy.

Then when I got into high school, and I went from a private grade school to Upper St. Clair High School, where I didn't know most of the people. It was in ninth grade that I began to realize just how useful being funny could be in everyday life, and largely through humor I could make friends, make the bullies laugh so they would leave me alone, became pretty popular and made friends with people I'm still close to today.

High school was when I really began performing in earnest, though it was not in any of the plays or usual productions of *Oklahoma!* that most aspiring show business people get involved in. While I secretly admired the kids who did act in plays, I preferred to hang back and good-naturedly make fun of them. Eventually, I was approached by Mr. Harshman, who oversaw the theater department. He said, "I hear you're a funny guy. Why don't you ever try out for any of the plays?" I told him I didn't want to seem snobbish but that I preferred to do my own material. Not to be cocky, but I think I'm much funnier than Rodgers and Hammerstein.

He found this amusing and told me that he was starting a program called "Traveling Troupe," which would consist of a group of students who would perform at various community functions. Mr. Harshman informed me that they had singers, dancers, guitarists, kids doing dramatic monologues, but no comedians. Right away, then, he'd appealed to something I'm always interested in: lack of competition. I agreed to work up a routine and join the troupe.

Courtesy Michael S. Schwartz/Getty.

All things considered, I enjoyed the experience. To actually have been introduced as a comedian to a group of people I didn't know, and to have more or less entertained them, made me feel like a real comedian. Mr. Harshman was encouraging, and when I reported to my parents that all had gone fairly well at the Elks Club, they were pleased. Eventually, I learned how to tweak jokes, how to deliver them, how to anticipate what would probably get a laugh and what probably wouldn't. By the time I graduated, I had become pretty comfortable on stage.

Where it really took off for me was as a freshman at Ohio State. My first day on campus,

I saw a sign in the student union that advertised an Amateur Comedy Contest. I decided I'd enter and once again was the only person doing original material. I won twenty-five dollars and immediate respect of my new roommates. This was the early '80s, and the so-called comedy boom was just beginning.

After moving back to Pittsburgh, I began to work regularly at a club called the Funny Bone. I was lucky enough to work with a wide assortment of great comedic talent such as Jay Leno, Paul Reiser, Steven Wright and Dennis Miller, also a Pittsburgh native who, by that time, was established as the big fish in the city.

Now that I was doing comedy professionally, I was constantly under pressure to create new material. By 1987, my stand-up had garnered me a lot of attention in Pittsburgh, and I was hired to do segments on the local CBS affiliate, KDKA TV. The station had an afternoon show called *Pittsburgh 2Day*, and I would appear with prop-oriented bits such as wacky gift suggestions for the holidays or bogus cooking segments. My best memory was getting to live out a fantasy when I shot a remote video segment about the opening of the baseball season. I got to put on a Pirates uniform and run around the turf at Three Rivers Stadium, this time without being chased out by security.

It was pretty shocking how quickly the career gravy train began flowing once Dennis Miller hired me to write on his new show, *Dennis Miller Live* on HBO. I loaded up my belongings in my Ford Escort and drove across the country. Dennis's show did a tremendous thing for me: it enabled me to win an Emmy, and when it was announced that I, along with my co-workers, had been nominated for the Emmy in the category of outstanding writing, I was completely dazed.

The greatest part of it all was the teary phone call I got to make to my parents back in Pittsburgh. It seemed that finally, all the heartache and struggle and sweat and toil paid off handsomely. And I was thrilled because they were thrilled. Even though they didn't always understand why I had to be in this business—I'm not sure I totally understood either—they were incredibly supportive, probably more so than I would have been in their situation. A few days later, I flew back to Pittsburgh and surprised my parents and sisters by bringing the Emmy with me.

By 1996, everything seemed to be going my way. It boggled my mind that I was being courted by agents who also represented some of the biggest names in the industry. In the back of my mind was often the thought: what is a kid from Pittsburgh doing here with these people? Maybe I should steal an ashtray to prove I was actually in the building.

GEORGE BENSON

We have grown used to seeing George Benson—an all-time icon and Grammy-winning giant of jazz—on stage due to his sky-high status. During a six-decade career marked by awards, acclaim and Billboard*-topping output, the Pittsburgh Hill District–born veteran has earned his place in both the history books and the biggest venues around the world. In 2009, Benson was recognized by the National Endowment of the Arts as a Jazz Master, the nation's highest honor in jazz.*

Pittsburgh had a lot of music when I was a kid. I lived near Wiley Avenue and Fulton Street. That was the mecca. Wiley was where a lot of musicians hung out when they came to Pittsburgh. They did their jamming right here in the Hill District. There was a club called the Stanley on one side, right across the street was the Blue Note, and they had Goode's Drug Store. That's where I played my ukulele right in front of there. I just turned around and started singing and playing. And a crowd formed around, and they all started going in their pockets. Then my cousin went around with his baseball cap, and boy, did we have money. We were rich. It was my first paying gig.

I never thought I would make it out of my teens. In my teens it was a rough period in my life. Lots of gangs, and we lost a lot of friends to gangs and wars. That ended when that started happening. We realized, "Hey, this stuff is serious. Our lives are at stake." We came to our senses and the gangs broke up. It's ever present in my mind. Now, I go back and I remember all the things they kept telling me: "George, you ain't never going to be nothing until you get out of here."

Pittsburgh was the last big stop before they made on their way to the Big Apple. Guys like Charlie Parker used to come through to try their chops out. Pittsburgh was also known for having some great musicians who came from there: Erroll Garner, Art Blakey and Billy Eckstine being the biggest.

When I was seven years old, I wanted to play guitar, but I was too small to handle it. I found a ukulele in the trash all smashed up, and my stepfather fixed it up, put some strings on it and taught me the first few chords I ever played. I went out and played for change on the corners, and years later Billy Eckstine told me, "Yeah, we used to give you quarters." I was seven years old and got to shake hands with Charlie Parker.

My stepfather was a guitar player, and when he got his amplifier out of the pawn shop, he plugged it in. And when he turned it on, that sound was like the most incredible thing I ever heard. I pressed my back against it, and the vibes went right through my chest, right through my body, and I was

Courtesy Frans Schelleken/
Redferns.

hooked on that sound. Like my ukulele, he later made my first guitar. We were impoverished in those days, and the electric guitar I wanted cost fifty-five dollars. It was in the pawn shop window, and I took him to see it and he said, "Man, you know I can make that." And he did. I drew the guitar on a piece of brown paper, and he traced it on a piece of oak wood and carved it with hacksaw blades. It took two days.

My repertoire is filled with all kinds of music. I was a jukebox kid. I'd copy whatever I heard on the jukebox. My mom was a singer, but she never did it professionally; she had to stop. She was only fifteen when she had me. But she sang all the time.

Pittsburgh was in the heart of everything. It was on the way to New York. With the Pennsylvania Turnpike a three-hundred-mile straight shot to the Big Apple, musicians would come to Pittsburgh to lock horns with all the baddest musicians in town. All those great jazz guys and musicians of all other kinds.

By my teen years, I had built a reputation as one of the city's best street musicians, but I was engaged to be married at age nineteen, needed a steadier income and found a job in home construction. That's when I reached a life-changing decision on one such home in Beaver Falls.

I had a hatchet in one hand and a hammer in another, and I thought to myself, "Boy, if I missed a nail or hit my hand with that axe I'd never play guitar again." So I dropped that axe and walked away. The foreman said, "Where do you think you're going?" and I said, "I'm sorry, but I can't do this anymore."

But as I was coming of age, the clubs and the neighborhood would fall victim to the wrecking ball as the Lower Hill was razed to make way for the Civic Arena. Our lives became fragmented. We became project people.

Nicer dwellings, yes, but no real character. I felt I had to leave, and in New York the release of the breakthrough album *Breezin'* combined jazz guitar with my voice. It changed my life, and it changed the world of jazz and pop music. It really was a landmark album.

When I first came to New York in 1963, I was playing guitar for Brother Jack McDuff's nationally touring soul-jazz trio. And McDuff was a no-nonsense guy. He was a very hard and tough bandleader. He forced me to do what I had not done before. I mean, I'm someone who can hear a song once and I know it. But he made me understand it, inside and out, to really get to know the harmony. We recorded an album at the Rudy Van Gelder studio there, and I fell in love with that studio. When I lived in Harlem, I used to cross the George Washington Bridge to record there for Blue Note and A&M sessions and ultimately my CTI sides. Rudy was a maverick; as far as engineering was concerned, he did everything himself. I made records with him for many years, including sides with Stanley Turrentine, Freddie Hubbard and people like that.

I see the progress Pittsburgh is making, and I like what I see. Nobody could love Pittsburgh more. I've seen what a town like this can produce. I saw the masters come through here when I was a little boy. I grew up poor but in a cradle of jazz. Pittsburgh was a mecca for both homegrown musicians and those passing through on their way to New York.

For a Pittsburgh homecoming, I always hope to get reacquainted with a few old haunts, such as Station Square. I love going into that old building. Just to step into that building and eat dinner near where the trains go by, that's a good feeling.

JEFF GOLDBLUM

Jeff Goldblum is an actor and jazz pianist. He has starred in more than seventy films, including Nashville, Annie Hall, Jurassic Park, The Big Chill *and* The Fly. *His latest jazz album is* The Capitol Studios Sessions.

I grew up in West Homestead, a suburb about twenty minutes southeast of Pittsburgh, where I projected a sunny personality, willing enthusiasm and playfulness. West Homestead was up in the hills, and our house was a brick Colonial. All of the kids in the neighborhood played in the street or in the woods nearby.

Courtesy Getty Images.

In our living room, we had a baby-grand Steinway. My mother, Shirley, knew her way around the keyboard, so we had lots of piano books. I used them to learn chord markings and how to improvise. I also played on our upright piano in the basement. It was the '60s, so I painted it lots of different colors.

I started taking piano lessons when I was ten. Like most kids, I studied classical music for the first couple of years. Then my teacher gave me sheet music to a song that became my gateway to jazz. The song was "The Alley Cat." Even though the pop instrumental from 1962 ended up a silly line-dance song at weddings, I was hooked on its piano syncopation.

When my father, Harold, listened to records, he gave me a music-appreciation lesson. For example, when pianist Erroll Garner was playing, my father would say, "Listen to this guy. He sits on a phone book. Listen how he pauses and what he does with octaves."

My father was a medical doctor who had a strong work ethic. When he was young, he flirted with the idea of being an actor. My mother was a homemaker who raised four kids with vigor and ferocity and verve. She was wondrous and youthful. Once all her kids grew up and left home, she went back to school and became a sex therapist. Then she became a local radio personality. She, too, had interest in becoming an actor early on.

In 1964, when Thelonious Monk was on the cover of *TIME* magazine, my older brother, Rick, played me one of his albums. I was amazed. My brother Rick was into jazz and loved the Modern Jazz Quartet, Stan Getz and Miles Davis.

At fifteen, I thought I could play for a paying audience. One day I locked myself in my room with the Yellow Pages. I went through the listings of Pittsburgh cocktail lounges. Then I called them. I'd say, "Hi, I understand you need a pianist." Most club managers were puzzled. They said, "We do? Well, we have a piano here. Why don't you come down and play." I got a couple of jobs that way. When I backed female singers, they drove me to gigs.

Even though I was practicing piano regularly, my dream was to become an actor. I first got romantic about being an actor because I saw plays growing up in Pittsburgh. I caught the bug, and I've had the best times, the most moving times, watching things on stage, and I was crazy enough to make this commitment to a lifelong marriage to acting. I was obsessed.

When I went to Chatham Music Day Camp, between fifth, sixth and seventh grades, that's when my world of curiosity and passion exploded. This group of people who were there just thrilled me. I had a flair for some of the things. There was arts-and-crafts, piano and music appreciation....The arts have changed my life. There was drama for the first time, which really made me decide that I wanted to be an actor. Then, between ninth and tenth and eleventh grades, I went to six-week sessions at Carnegie Mellon University. That's when I *really* became obsessed with being an actor.

My first play was *Belle of the Balkans* in summer camp. It was a spoof of a Gilbert and Sullivan operetta. I played the lead character. It was a little musical, and I acted and rehearsed it and then leaped on stage. My dad had said, "If you find something you love to do, that's a compass and a lighthouse and a guide toward what your vocation might be."

I wore plaid shorts and had a camera around my neck. The audience laughed a bit, and I was exhilarated. That night, I remember my parents were in the audience. After I came off, they said, "How'd you like that?" I went, "I did. I *did*!" That's all I said, but I think I had already decided for myself: *I want to be an actor.* Then when I took that Carnegie Mellon course, I was wildly obsessed with it. Every day before I went to school, I took a shower with this glass door, and it would steam up and I'd write, "Please, God, let me be an actor." And then before I left, I would wipe it off. Acting became a passionate obsession; I was just driven.

The first adult shows I remember were at the Nixon. "Beyond the Fringe" was the first sophisticated, adult thing. I remember getting sweaty, thinking, "I'm going to jump up and get involved in the show!" I didn't, but it was a close thing. I was stage-struck. We used to see live shows at the Leona Theater. There's nothing as powerful as live theater, the innocence and poetry of it.

I applied to Carnegie Mellon in my senior year, but they rejected me. So I moved to New York to study with Sanford Meisner at the Neighborhood Playhouse. I lived in a box of an apartment at Sutton Place on East 57th Street. During my second year, I quit the Playhouse. I had landed a part in the chorus of *Two Gentlemen of Verona* on Broadway in 1971.

In 1973, I auditioned in New York for a movie. About fifty tough-looking guys were waiting to read for the director. We went into the room three at a time. I wound up playing a home invader in *Death Wish*.

I continued to play piano. I found Frank Cunimondo, a Pittsburgh jazz pianist and teacher. At the time, he had two albums out—*Communication* and

The Lamp Is Low. My parents drove me to his house, and I took lessons. Frank showed me more advanced chords and new ways to improvise. Then I went to see him play at local gigs.

I perform jazz almost every Wednesday at Rockwell in Los Angeles. When we played Hollywood Bowl a couple of decades ago, we didn't have a name yet. It was for the Playboy Jazz Festival. They said, "We've got to put something on the program." I remembered this lady from Pittsburgh, Mildred Snitzer...it was funny and it stuck, so I perform as a jazz pianist with the Mildred Snitzer Orchestra.

The guys I'm playing with now for the last ten years are some of the best jazz musicians in the world. You'll hear some jazz '50s, '60s Blue Note kind of stuff, some Thelonious Monk, Herbie Hancock...there's some singing involved, but I keep it loose. We play games with the audience, questions and answers, trivia, all manner of movie talk.

My playing and acting inform each other, especially when it comes to improvisation. Jazz and acting have a lot in common, I think.

I'm a Steelers fan and never miss a snap. I rise and fall with every game. I want to come back this next year, I want to see a Steelers game, I want to go to the Andy Warhol Museum and I want to go to the Carnegie Museum.

JOE NEGRI

Joseph Harold Negri is one of the most recognized names in Pittsburgh music circles and is one of the finest jazz guitarists in the country. He was a musical prodigy at age four and was touring nationally by the age of sixteen. He appeared as himself and as "Handyman Negri" in the Neighborhood of Make-Believe segments on Mister Rogers' Neighborhood.

In 1999, the Pittsburgh Cultural Trust honored me by naming me the "Established Artist of the Year." I remember telling them that my career has been a "work in progress" since age three.

As a child performer, I performed on radio and appeared in theatrical and stage productions throughout the tri-state area. I was even chosen to become one of Pittsburgh's "Stars of Tomorrow." A voice change shattered my confidence, and I stopped performing. Shortly after, I began to seriously study the guitar.

When I reached a certain age, my brother and my cousin, we both went to dancing school. I would sing a song, and then we would tap dance. I think it was the hope and dream of many parents during the 1930s that their children, if they had musical talent, they would make it to Hollywood. We were hard-pressed for money, and many child performers were making it big in Hollywood, people like Shirley Temple, Jackie Cooper and Judy Garland.

WE MADE MONEY FOR our families during the Depression. By age sixteen, I was playing well enough to win a job with one of the country's top swing bands. I soon became a featured member of the band and traveled nationally with them for about two years. Though the army briefly sidetracked my career, it by no means stopped it. I was fortunate enough to meet up with several top-notch jazz musicians, and together we continued to develop our musical skills.

In the early '50s, I enrolled at Carnegie Tech, and I picked up some important musical training and overall grooming, a lot of stuff growing up—pop, jazz—and I knew about harmony. But I had never had any real formal training. Carnegie Tech molded me and helped me to put all of that into perspective. I found out why all these things happened. I learned about harmony and counterpoint. It was like this great awakening. School also taught me to express myself and to become a better-rounded person.

I feel very strongly that these years rounded me as a person and prepared me for the work that was still to come. Following Carnegie, I landed a job in the "brand new" media of television. It was the start of a forty-year career. My TV work began at KDKA-TV, where I headed up my own trio, and following that, I spent some twenty years at WTAE-TV as an "on the air performer" and musical director.

Courtesy Wikimedia Commons.

It was during this time that I met, feel in love with and married Joni Serafini. Shortly after that, Joni and I began to seriously consider moving to NYC, even though my career was beginning to take shape here in Pittsburgh. New York City has always been the mecca for artists, and music was no exception. The recording studios, the major radio stations and major TV networks represented the

"Holy Grail" of the music business in the middle of the last century. Our first daughter, Lisa, was born a few years after we were married. A year or so later, we decided that we should look into opportunities in the Big Apple!

We visited with several musician friends, and we surveyed the music scene closely. Even though the opportunities seemed abundant, I noted that living wasn't easy in New York. The kids had babysitters. Somebody had to take them to the park to play. The whole scene just kind of turned me off. So we packed up and chose to return to Pittsburgh. The thought of raising Lisa and a family in that environment discouraged any ideas of becoming a New York studio musician.

Life has a strange way of working things out. It came to pass that the studios were to undergo a revolutionary transformation. The '60s brought great changes to the recording industry and the TV studios. We have never regretted our decision to return to Pittsburgh.

My current professional bio states that I'm one of the most recognized names in Pittsburgh music circles and perhaps one of the best jazz guitarists in the country. I started playing the guitar when I was eight years old.

As one wit remarked, "Joe Negri was playing the guitar long before it was fashionable." My life, in many ways, parallels the history of the jazz guitar. I grew up listening to and emulating guitarists like Charlie Christian, Les Paul and Django Reinhart. I consider myself to be a part of the second wave of jazz guitarists that came into prominence after World War II. Some of my peers included Johnny Smith, Jimmy Raney, Wes Montgomery, Tal Farlow, Herb Ellis, Barney Kessel, Joe Pass and Kenny Burrell. I always felt I needed a little more support—a horn or a piano, or something.

I'm known to millions of children for my appearances as "Handyman Negri" on the PBS show *Mister Rogers' Neighborhood*. That is a role I have played for over thirty years. I had never done any acting, so I was a little nervous about that initially, but Fred Rogers was great and I quickly became at ease with it because I decided to just be myself. I also got an opportunity to play a little on the music shop.

I'll never forget, with Fred we had a big joke about that. 'Cause I said to him, "Handyman? You've gotta be kidding." He said, "Don't worry about it, it's pretend." So I pretended my way to being a handyman. My wife is actually handier than I am! She can fix things; she's really good at it.

As a composer, I have written music for many documentary film scores. In addition, my credits include *The Crossing* (scored for Brass Band and Jazz Trio). I wrote my first guitar method book, an introduction to improvisation entitled *A Common Sense Approach to Guitar Improvisation*. I had my studio gig. So what I was going to get in New York I got here! And I still had a family and was making a decent living. It's been a very rewarding career.

I'm still a work in progress. There are many musical things I want to accomplish. Music has never been an easy business, but I honestly wouldn't change it for anything in the world. So, the "work in progress" continues on in the twenty-first century. I pray that the music continues and that I continue to write, teach and perform as long as I am able to do so with style and grace.

JOE SAYLOR

Joe Saylor is a musician based in New York City. He is the "Jazz Cowboy" with his signature black cowboy hat and currently plays with Jon Batiste and Stay Human, the house band on The Late Show with Stephen Colbert.

I was born and raised in Indiana, Pennsylvania, and both my mother and father are musicians and their primary job has been serving in the public schools. My dad was a choir director and a band director for thirty years, and my mother was a choir director for a local high school. So music has been a part of my life from the very beginning. My parents actually met in the IUP marching band in college, so they love marching bands and drum corps so they would take us to see a lot of marching bands when we were young.

Our family was also involved in our church, and my dad was an arranger for the music ministry and I actually started playing drums in church. We always had music playing in the house, whether we were listening to records, CDs or my parents teaching private music lessons. At home we listened to a lot of big band jazz, drum corps and contemporary Christian music. My dad played recordings of people like Maynard Ferguson, Woody Herman, Harry Connick Jr., Phil Driscoll and Ron Kenoly.

When I was twelve years old, I started listening heavily to more of what you would call bop/hard-bop/post-bop jazz. That took me through my teenage years, and when I moved to New York City in 2004, my ears were exposed even further to all kinds of sounds ranging from electronica to opera to avant-garde music. While studying at the Juilliard School, the late Phil Schaap deepened my listening experience with early jazz and American roots music.

I feel like I had extra favor having a dad that was a lover of music and as involved in the community as he was because he taught at the various local schools, and anytime there was an opportunity to involve me in something he

Courtesy Rahev Segev.

would take it. I remember he would direct the high school jazz band, and they would have evening rehearsals. Whenever their drummer couldn't be there, he would bring me in to play with the high school band and other opportunities to play around town at a young age.

My parents were so important to me musically for sure but also as people… they always put family and my interests first.

My drive to become a jazz musician started when my father took me to see Roger Humphries, Pittsburgh's great jazz drummer who's played with folks like Dizzy Gillespie and Ray Charles. Roger was the single greatest musical influence for me, and at the time he was hosting a weekly jam session on Tuesday nights at the James Street Tavern so my dad would go and see them. He told Roger that "I have a twelve year old boy that is talented, would you be interested in teaching him?" Roger said to bring me to the jam session and "We'll see what he's got."

Well, that night completely changed my life. From the minute I walked into that club, I knew I wanted to play jazz. Roger changed my life. Afterward, he said, "Bring him by the house on Saturday." That was the start of a seven-year-long relationship and mentorship.

Being around Roger focused my sights on where I wanted to go musically speaking. He introduced me to the music of Art Blakey, Stanley Turrentine, Horace Silver, John Coltrane and so many others that would have a profound impact on me as a musician. My mom and dad were musicians and lovers of music and exposed me to a lot of things, but Roger really showed me this other world of jazz that I was unaware of. He would tell me stories about Billy Eckstein, Art Blakey and Errol Garner, and I felt like, at twelve and thirteen years old, I was being brought into and initiated into this amazing culture.

Pittsburgh is right up there in the top five of great jazz cities in America. I saw Take Six, Wynton Marsalis, Harry Connick Jr., so many others, and when I was in high school, I also had the opportunity to play with the Pittsburgh Symphony at Heinz Hall, which was amazing.

After graduating from Indiana Area High School, I set off on my pursuit of a career in jazz. I earned a bachelor's at Manhattan School of Music then later my master's at Juilliard School. I was able to hold down the drum chair for about two years with Vince Giordano and the Nighthawks Orchestra. They are the preeminent jazz band interpreting the music of the 1920s and 1930s. That experience also had a lasting influence on me.

What helped me get to where I am today was the hard work ethic in Western Pennsylvania; people looked out for each other, and they were loyal. That's another thing I found out about Pittsburgh—people are very loyal. That has definitely affected me and is something that I was very adamant about carrying with me in my work and with friends and family when I moved to New York.

The skills I have developed may have earned a lot of people's admiration, but I don't want to get distracted by that. I want to focus on uniting and uplifting people with my art and talent. Anytime that I play music for people and it touches them and uplifts them in a certain way, that's always the best feeling for me, to know that I have that kind of impact. My goal is to uplift and love people through music.

KEN GARGARO

For nearly half a century, teaching youngsters about the performing arts has been a daily mission for Ken Gargaro, the founding director of Pittsburgh Musical Theater. In addition to being a theater entrepreneur, Gargaro has been a producer and director and recently had the Gargaro Theater in Pittsburgh's West End dedicated in his honor.

On the night of my birth, September 28, 1948, at Magee Women's Hospital, my father, Tony, was playing trumpet at a gig at the Islam Grotto on Pittsburgh's North Side, near what is now Acrisure Stadium. Music illuminated my life from that day forward. Although Tony gave up professional music shortly thereafter to join Rust Engineering as a mechanical engineer, he continued to play trumpet. Sunday afternoon rehearsals in Norwood, at my dad's side with the Villetta Barrea Band at the VB club, figure prominently as one of my earliest memories.

Norwood, along with West Park, Stowe Township and the Bottoms, over which Norwood hovered, comprised McKees Rocks (every area in Pittsburgh has several names). In the 1950s, this area was a thriving center of Italian American immigrant culture. The band, associated with the VB Club, played ubiquitous Italian festivals in such neighborhoods as Oakland, Morningside, East Liberty and Bloomfield. Each festival ran for several days and included street music, giant dancing dolls, fireworks and a

Courtesy Ken Gargaro.

traveling Madonna to which members of the community attached dollar bills.

My grandparents, brewery workers with a strong work ethic, honored music, both instrumental and vocal, as a sign of cultural refinement. Both paternal [Gargaro] and maternal [Rubino] aunts, uncles and cousins sang or played an instrument. If you came to a party at my house, you would dance the Tarantella and sing Neapolitan folk songs with a band accompaniment. These first influences proved powerful and led me to classical training in music education at Duquesne University.

One Sunday afternoon in my junior year (1968) at the Lowe's Penn on Sixth (now Heinz Hall), a performance of *Man of La Mancha*, starring Richard Kiley, transformed me from a musician who wanted to be a high school music teacher into a musician devoted to the passionate intensity of musicals. The theater bug had bitten.

My first real job was in 1970 as choral director for Plum High School, where I also directed my first musical, *Bye Bye Birdie*. In the evenings after teaching, I began acting at the White Barn Theatre, Pittsburgh Playhouse and West Hills Community Theatre and attending shows at the Odd Chair Playhouse. I shared my passion for musicals with student groups by sponsoring field trips to see the first concert performance of *Jesus Christ Superstar* at the Civic Arena and a professional production of *Fiddler on the Roof* at the Pittsburgh Playhouse. Higher education occupied the balance of the 1970s, which culminated in a successful defense of my dissertation, "Bob Fosse and the Translation of Musicals to the Screen," at the University of Pittsburgh on September 28, 1979, my thirty-first birthday.

I went on to become an assistant professor at Western Maryland College. But when my hometown beckoned, I answered. I was hired by Point Park College in 1982 with the challenge of resurrecting the Playhouse School, a community education outlet. The Playhouse School classes were held in an old house on the corner of Forbes and Craft Avenues. Unused for ten years, with paint peeling off the exterior and the bathroom lights not working, I embraced the space as a gift. My thirteen-year-old daughter Katie told me it looked like a firetrap.

I also developed a curriculum for a musical theater major for Point Park College, which at this point owned the Playhouse. The classroom became a testing ground for my theory that "continuity of training that was tested regularly in performance" could shape careers. My dream to direct a show there led to my directing/musically directing *1940s Radio Hour* in 1983. That show became the biggest hit the Playhouse had seen in decades. This success led to producing and directing the Playhouse Professional Company on a regular basis, thus providing a capstone for students, to secure access to side-by-side performance opportunities with seasoned professionals.

A reinvigorated Playhouse celebrated its fiftieth anniversary with the first regional production of *A Chorus Line* in 1985, directed by a youthful Danny Herman, a local boy from McKees Rocks who was a veteran of the Broadway production. The show starred Fosse protégé Lenora Nemetz, a Pittsburgher fresh off stints in the original production of *Chicago*, and featured then college students Rob Ashford, now a successful international director, and Tony Award winner Kathleen Marshall in lead roles. I supervised rehearsals and conducted the orchestra.

But it was the producing of the regional premiere of *Little Shop of Horrors* in 1986 that put the Playhouse on the map as an "Off Broadway"–style house like the Orpheum in NYC. An all-student cast, along with professional Richard Rauh, who played Mr. Mushnik, proved my belief that the Point Park/Playhouse synergy could nurture Broadway careers through apprenticeships that allowed students to work alongside professionals. Linda Gabler (Audrey) from Burgettstown and Tom Rocco (Seymour) from the North Side became Broadway veterans.

In 1990, I founded Gargaro Productions to further this vision. *Beehive*, an Off Broadway show I had seen in the late '80s, became our first major success in 1992. Etta Cox, Sandy Dowe, Rema Webb, Maria Beacoates Bey, Sharon (Connelly) Schaller, Danny Herman, Tammy (Flodine) Wyatt and other major hometown professionals displayed what we could do with Yinzer talent. The 1993 through 1995 seasons chugged along nicely with audiences and reputation building. Gargaro Productions expanded into a four-show season at the Fulton (Byham) Theater in the Cultural District with around 4,500 subscribers, mostly families looking for an affordable way to introduce their kids to musicals.

In 1996, timing was right to expand into a two-week run. We were on our way to becoming a force in Pittsburgh. The venerable Don Brockett said, "I understand what you are doing." Such an imprimatur encouraged me. The next step was to establish a musical theater educational program to complement the professional productions.

Richard Rauh, through a generous donation, bankrolled a conservatory for young students, ages seven to eighteen, in tandem with the professional company in that same year. One of the everlasting joys of my personal commitment to education through musical theater became the never-ending parade of talented Pittsburgh kids with whom I crossed paths. Providing opportunities for Pittsburgh youth was integral to my vision. Many went on to Broadway careers, and some returned to Gargaro to perform locally. Billy Porter, whom I first met at Pittsburgh's High School for the Creative and Performing Arts, always stepped up when called upon.

In 1983, I developed and directed a showcase for talent at CAPA, then located in Homewood. Sophomore Billy Porter drove that show by singing tunes from Prince's *Purple Rain*. In 1989, while at CMU, he starred as Jimmy Early for the Pittsburgh premiere of *Dreamgirls* at the Playhouse, a show I musically directed. In 1997, he directed *The Wiz* for Gargaro Productions and wrote a new song called "Emerald City" for the show. In 2000, he flew in from L.A. for a weekend of performances of *Sophisticated Ladies*. His solo singing in Pittsburgher Billy Strayhorn's *Lush Life* stopped the show. At Soldiers & Sailors Hall in 2003, he nailed two gospel numbers from *Civil War*, which I directed. Now a Tony, Emmy and Grammy Award winner, I celebrate Billy as a local kid that was generous with his talent.

Gargaro Productions was renamed Pittsburgh Musical Theater in 2001 to reflect its reality as a nonprofit company devoted to musical theater and the community. I retired several years later at age seventy, confident in the sustainability of my vision to foster the genre of musical theater production and education with local talent. Reflecting on my career, I can now see how the values of the immigrant community in which I was raised and my musical heritage preordained my career and devotion to the Pittsburgh community.

MARIA CARUSO

Maria Angelica Caruso is an American-born dancer, choreographer, academic, social activist, fitness and wellness practitioner and entrepreneur whose enterprise encompasses brand models focused in the arts, education, entertainment and wellbeing sectors. Caruso's dance business comprises five performance companies, a dance conservatory, a fitness program and a dance movement therapy system, all under the umbrella of the Bodiography brand.

I owe Pittsburgh everything, really. I lived most of my early life in Rural Valley, near Kittanning, and was drawn to dance before I was three. In sixth grade, I met Luba Takamoto, with whom I have kept in touch with over the years. She told me after my audition, "Your technique is challenged, but you have a lot of passion. I can take you under my wing and make you a dancer."

I danced twelve hours a week. It was like therapy for me. I loved the academic perspective too. She gave me a workbook from which I learned all the French ballet words. That's when I gained great respect for the art form and its history. I modeled my dance school after that experience because I felt it was incredibly valuable.

In high school, I took part in an experimental program which allowed me to take college courses. I had a strong interest in medicine and wanted for a while to be a doctor. But when it was time to enroll in college, dance was my whole focus. As far as education and attending a university, I wanted to go to the most distant place possible. I felt like I needed a bigger city, a bigger vibe. I checked out various schools and picked Florida State University in Tallahassee and got off to a fast start, performing in both classical and contemporary works on the same show as a freshman.

I was a sponge for dance in college, even traveling to New York City one summer for an intensive program at the Dance Theater of Harlem. I was known for my extensions and could take my leg to my ear, but my body was changing. As I grew as a woman and became more voluptuous, I no longer fit the stereotype of a ballet dancer, even though I weighed 115 pounds.

While in college, I was clear with myself that I never wanted to come back to Pittsburgh, never be director of a dance company, never wanted to own a dance school and never wanted to be a choreographer. I just wanted to be a dancer. But after college, when I was in New York City to further my career, I got some free studio space and decided maybe it would be a good idea to get some friends together, start a company and start workshopping material.

Courtesy Eric Rose.

I started Bodiography in New York, and more than twenty years ago, I made the decision to take the company to Pittsburgh. I feel like this was my calling to go back and honor where I came from and what really motivated me to create Bodiography. When I look back, I would never change anything in my life, but it was really my dad who kept telling me to come back to Pittsburgh. I started to realize that Pittsburgh is about its people, it's the community, it's about nurturing that, and in every situation I had I went full circle. It provides me with the opportunity to create new ballets, teach dance and exercise and create a positive self-image for people who don't fit the stereotype of a ballet dancer's body.

There are so many hidden treasures here that I didn't even know existed. That's why Pittsburgh is so special. Integrity, commitment, hardworking, dedication…those are all the things that when I grew up were instilled in me. My coal mining family was hardworking and super loving. I wasn't going to work in a steel mill, but I took those values and applied them to what I wanted to do in life.

I know from other large dance companies that I've worked with a lot of people have commented on how I treat my company like a family, and that's a very inviting thing. There are traditions that I've adopted and carried into my professional life. My first show in New York I had a cookie table. The church ladies went to New York with my grandparents with an entire truck load of cookies because we had to have a cookie table at my first show. If that isn't Pittsburgh, I don't know what is. The support system of being together, the togetherness factor, and treating each other like family—those are qualities that make Pittsburgh a one-of-a-kind place.

It's like *Mister Roger's Neighborhood*. Community is such a huge part of the culture and how we are efficient at being disciplined and working; it's about that balance. I think being in other places in the world and recognizing how different it was made Pittsburgh all that more special. Sometimes it takes being away from it to recognize it. I wanted to be away, but then I understood how special it was, and coming back was the best decision that I ever made.

MICHAEL CAMPAYNO

Michael Campayno originated the role of Rob Camilletti in The Cher Show *and also starred as Fiyero in the hit musical* Wicked *on Broadway. A graduate of Carnegie Mellon School of Drama, he made his television debut as Rolf in the NBC live telecast of* The Sound of Music *starring Carrie Underwood and can be heard on the cast recording.*

My story starts with a torn rotator cuff. I am the youngest of six kids, and all of my brothers and sisters dabbled in theater. I always loved theater, but I never thought that I could really pursue it. I was a swimmer for ten to twelve years, and I was like, "This is it. I love swimming. This is perfect." It was just so much work, and in high school we could swim at like 4:00 a.m. before school and then we could swim after school, too, and have meets. And I just couldn't handle it.

I then kind of had a *High School Musical*/Troy Bolton moment when I injured my shoulder. With no ticket to the Olympics and nothing to lose, I started down a new path. My sophomore year of high school I was going to try out for the play. My shoulder was busted, so I said I'm just going to try out for the musical. I was so nervous. I never even sang before really, and I wasn't one of those child prodigies.

It turns out, during my senior year of high school, I won a Gene Kelly Award for Best Supporting Actor, an award that highlights high school musical theater excellence in Pittsburgh. I won this award, and I was like, "Oh, maybe I could do this for real."

I went to Carnegie Mellon School of Drama, and the minute I arrived I felt like I was asked so many things about who I was and my opinions and all that stuff. It really forced me to grow up and become an individual. The acting program is so demanding and so structured, but it's what you need to do because it totally prepares you for any performance style out there.

The summer of my senior year, I started working with my manager, and he got me this audition for *The Sound of Music Live!* Nobody knew what it was. We just heard "live," and we were like, "What does it mean? Is it live, like people are going to be there? Are they filming it? Is it a concert?"

I went through about three months and eight demanding callbacks. They kept pairing us with different girls and calling us back in for different people. We basically did the whole "Sixteen Going On Seventeen" scene and dance.

Courtesy Susan Shacter.

But yes, I booked the job. Funnily enough, I was doing *The Crucible* at Carnegie Mellon at night, so my final callback was for the producers in the morning in New York. I flew back and did *The Crucible*, and then I found out I booked it, which was amazing.

After landing the role of Rolf, I just left school, which was a crazy decision too.… It was really hard. My family was really upset, and I was just in between two places because I wanted to get my degree but I stayed in New York and took jobs as they came. I wanted to have a Broadway credit   it was just a goal of mine—and my chance came when I was asked to audition for the role of Fiyero in *Wicked*, which indeed became my Broadway debut.

It was crazy. It was a lot of years of working really hard. You dream so much about it that you never know; it feels so out of reach, I guess. I actually don't even remember my opening night until I took my final bow. I had thirty members of my family there. They're all super supportive, and they love theater. I had a lot of my aunts and uncles there, and my grandparents were there. I actually didn't regain consciousness until I was taking my bow! I saw everybody standing up. It was so overwhelming. It was a huge overwhelming moment of gratitude for all the people that have supported me. It was crazy. I think about it a lot.

Theater is hard. It's intense and it's hard. My parents are always like, "You only work three hours a night," and I am like, yes, but my whole day is surrounded by the performance. If we are under the weather or anything, we have to take care of ourselves. It's so challenging.

You rehearse a very short amount of time. You just have to really be on your game. I would say the nostalgia, I feel like, of Broadway is so lovely. It's just truly a dream to walk down to work every night and pass all those marquees. I pass *School of Rock, Chicago, Cats*…just walking into that community and being a part of it is…I'm just so grateful. The feeling in the community is so supportive. That's one thing you just can't get anywhere else. I talk to people in Los Angeles and Chicago, and there's just a special environment and community that's been built for many years on Broadway. I feel like everybody just recognizes that and is very grateful to be in that community. That's very different.

So unwinding is important. I love Domino's. That's my guilty pleasure. I love bookstores and coffee shops. They are kind of my thing. I just like to go and browse in bookstores, and I love finding new coffee shops. It makes me feel comfortable. It's my aesthetic, and it really helps me focus back on me and what is outside of the show because it can always feel that you are just bombarded by whatever show you are in, *The Cher Show*, whatever, because you live there basically. Our dressing rooms are an extension of our apartments.

I can't stay away from Pittsburgh. I have only had a couple of days off, and I am already back. Pittsburgh is amazing. It's where my family is and where I have grown up. It's what I know. I am so proud to go to New York and say, "This is where I came from. This is what I know." And there are plenty more amazing people coming from where I just came from.

ROB MARSHALL

Rob Marshall is an American theater director, film director and choreographer. He is a six-time Tony Award nominee, Academy Award nominee, Golden Globe nominee and six-time Emmy winner whose most noted work is the Academy Award Best Picture winner Chicago. *His accomplishments have earned him a place in the Taylor Allderdice High School Hall of Fame, from which he graduated in 1978.*

I had no sense that I would end up in film, for sure. It all happened organically. I started in the chorus, and it was that classic trajectory because I didn't have a sense of that. Pittsburgh was an amazing place to grow up for me, because my parents are spectacular people. They showed me so much and opened my eyes to so much that was happening in Pittsburgh at the time. There is the Pittsburgh Opera, the Pittsburgh Ballet, the Public Theater and the Civic Light Opera, which was huge for me. And, of course, there was the arts everywhere here, and I was just exposed to so much that I felt it was a mini New York, because of its opportunities and anything was possible.

I started at Pittsburgh Civic Light Opera when I was a kid. I was in *The Sound of Music* there and *The King and I.* My parents loved musicals, and I don't know specifically what it was but I wanted to be a dancer and a singer and an actor. The music theater program at Carnegie Mellon was in its third year. Holly Hunter is two years older than me; she was a junior when I was a freshman.

It was an incredible program because there was no such thing like it anywhere in the country. Boston University had a great theater program, NYU, but here there was musical theater, which is what I wanted to do. And I wanted to dance. And when you're young, it's like an athlete—you want to dance now.

I took advantage of what was here. I wanted to do it and so much so that in my junior year I auditioned for the show *A Chorus Line,* and I got the show and left Carnegie for a year. I was on the road, Michael Bennett hired me and I came back for my senior year, which was nice because I could join my class again. They gave me credit for the full year. I remember opening my report card or something and I was in

Courtesy Jay Brooks.

San Francisco lounging in my apartment, and I thought, "Oh, that's nice." But in an odd way, I learned more my senior year after being out in the professional world and coming back and saw what I needed to work on, what I needed to focus on, and I really took advantage of Carnegie that year, very much so.

Working on new material was something we did a lot at Carnegie Mellon and in the process expressing yourself, learning who you are and what you are. I felt that I was supported in a big way to be myself and learn my craft. Because it was all here; we we're sort of learning how it all works together too....It was not as cohesive as it is now, it was a bit departmental. You would go to the music building and so on. But because it was all happening at once, it was perfect for me, especially the acting program, which is so strong. I could do ballet one minute, then acting the next, then vocals...it was a wonderful combination that I couldn't find anywhere else and at this level.

I was ready in a way because as a dancer, like I said, I was nineteen and really ready to dance. That's the height of your career in way as a dancer, so I was excited to get out there and do it. I really found out what it's like, and at the time *A Chorus Line* was kind of *the* show, it would be like getting *The Book of Mormon* now or something...it was a hot show.

I loved when I would audition as a dancer and you would walk in with hundreds of kids. But if you got past that, I would get to the singing part and I could sing, and that was very rare for a dancer. Then I would get to the reading and I could act because I had training, and I could put it all together.

My first Broadway show was *Zorba* with Anthony Quinn, and that's where I met Graciela Daniele, who was an incredible director and choreographer. She choreographed *Zorba*, and she asked me to do the next show, which was *The Rink*, which starred Liza Minnelli and Chita Rivera. And I was the dance captain at twenty-three years of age, and that's when I started to learn about being on the other side of the table and get a sense of how you put together a show.

Chita Rivera was our patron saint of musical theater, and she taught me so much about discipline, how you work in the theater and how you respect it. It was this huge learning experience because it's your life and it has to become something that you love.

As a film director, I feel that I am there to serve everybody. That's what I wanted to do and what I've always done. I'm there to serve people, to make you feel great, to have an incredible experience, and that's when the best work gets done. You're hired for your taste and your sensibilities, and that comes from who you are and what you love, what you watch, what inspired you, what inspired you as a kid. I was so lucky, I grew up going to the incredible productions of Michael Bennett, Bob Fosse, Gower Champion… those are my champions on stage, and on film Annie Doona, Robert Wise, Vincent Minnelli, George Cukor—those are my heroes. They brought me so much and I try to stay open to what the world is today, but it really comes from what you love.

I was very lucky. My first film won an Oscar for Best Picture, which is insane. And all of a sudden I had final cut, which is what you get when you get there. So I was in this incredibly envious position where I could make those kinds of decisions.

What challenges and inspires me now is I watch TCM, I watch old movies; they inspire me more than today's movies. For me, I find them more inspiring. I think the stories are so much stronger in many ways, the performances stronger in so many ways. Of course, there are movies that you love now, and there are a few great directors, Woody Allen being one of them.

The role my parents played meant everything…everything, because they let me dream, they let me be myself, they didn't judge me. It was an incredible experience. I think it was because my father was adopted as a child; he lost his parents when he was quite young and felt like he never really had a childhood. So with us, it was sort of like he was the fourth child in a way. It was a beautiful thing. They got married really young and they are still so incredibly vital, still live here in Pittsburgh, and they gave me the positive reinforcement that I try to give to others when I work with them.

FRANK NICOTERO

Frank Joseph Nicotero is an American stand-up comedian, television writer and television host. He is best known for hosting the game show Street Smarts, *which aired in syndication from 2000 to 2005.*

I was born in Beaver Falls…my dad was a DJ at a radio station up there WBVP, and that's where he became friends with Donnie Iris because Donnie was in the Jaggerz and he actually wrote a novelty song with the Jaggerz called "The Streaker." I consider the north hills my home, grew up in McCandless Township, went to Carson Middle School and North Allegheny High School, so I'm a North Allegheny guy, proud of it.

I remember when my dad took us to the Allegheny Center Mall and bought me my first Steelers shirt, it was 3/4 length, which was very in style in the late '70s, and I wore that thing like five times a week. My mom would have to pull it off of me...I loved it so much. I just remember I thought that people would only wear Steelers gear during football season but discovered as a kid that they wear it all the time, so I loved that I could

Courtesy Talent Network.

wear my Steelers shirt in the summer. I remember watching the Steelers play and had pictures of Lynn Swann and Terry Bradshaw up in my room. Sports were a really big and important thing for me, and I don't think you can grow up in a better sports town with the community rallying around teams the way Pittsburgh does.

In 1982, my dad was working on WDSY, the country radio station that I think now is Y108, and he got switched to overnight, and this movie called *Night Shift* came out with Henry Winkler. We didn't know Michael Keaton at the time, but we went to see it because my dad said, "I'm starting the night shift on Monday so let's go see this movie." So seeing *Night Shift* in a theater and learning that Michael Keaton was from Pittsburgh I went, "Well, wait a second, I can do that." He became my hero and idol, and it really set me on my career path because I wanted to be a comedian. I said, "Hey a guy from Pittsburgh did this so why can't I?"

You know, Carnegie Mellon is always the jumping-off point when I meet a lot of actors in Los Angeles. I was doing audience warm-ups for an NBC TV show called *Hollywood Game Night*, hosted by Jane Lynch, and Jeff Goldblum was a guest one day. And I said, "Hey, Jeff, I'm from Pittsburgh," and he immediately wanted to talk. I just wanted to talk about the Steelers with him, and his eyes lit up. The director said, "We're coming back from a commercial break," and Jeff Goldblum said, "No wait, one more minute," and he wanted to tell another story about the Steelers before they could shoot the rest of the show.

Pittsburgh has values that never left me, and I think it's saying Pittsburgh Pride, and it's such a hackneyed thing, but that's what one producer would say: "No one ever wants to talk about their hometown more than you when

Pittsburgh comes up." And then one day he calls me and he's with Billy Gardell. He says, "I'm sitting here with Billy Gardell," and Billy and I have known each other for years. After teasing me all these years, he tells me, "Billy won't shut up and stop talking about Pittsburgh as fucking much as you. I don't know what it is about you guys from Pittsburgh…maybe it's just comedians, it's all you guys want to talk about."

There's something about the pride, the blue-collar mentality. With Pittsburgh, it's because every family struggled, it's blue-collar, nine to five, working in the mill, and it's family infused there with pockets of Italian and Polish and others. People bonded so much from being from the tough city that really pulled itself out of the smoky era, cleaned itself up and became the Most Livable City in the early '80s. I think it's a pride thing for Pittsburghers.

Those values helped me to get where I am today. Being nice to people, greet people with a smile. I'm very open to talk to strangers, and I think that's a Pittsburgh thing, being very helpful. You hear stories about people breaking down on the parkway, and there's three or four cars that will stop to try and help them. You don't see that in other cities. You learn to be nice, and you learn to treat everybody like family. That's the beauty of Pittsburgh: it is a small town and you learn to be nice. I remember when Pittsburgh was named the nicest city in America, and it was true.

And the word *hon*. I remember taking somebody back home with me, and they couldn't understand what the word *hon* was all about, how everyone was called "hon" and they didn't get it. How everyone just greets you friendly. It's such a term of endearment, but it's such a Pittsburgh thing…you don't get "hon" in any other city. I've traveled all over this country, and it's just one of the nicest cities…people are just so warm and friendly there. Like the city went through such a battle to rebrand itself from the Steel City to this great city that people take pride in it. When I walk into a restaurant in the strip district and they say "Hi hon," it's like okay, I'm home. We should be grateful that we're from this great city.

I would have to say family is what influenced me the most. Look, I love my friends and all my best friends are still in Pittsburgh, but family is where you learn everything. My dad came from a big Italian family, and my mom is German and she was affected immediately. We would go to these family gatherings, and it's big and it's loud, and I was actually frightened of some of my older relatives because they were so loud and big. But family…my sister and I are still close, we talk on the phone about friends, play Wordle and talk smack. I think it all starts with family, and it's an important thing in Pittsburgh.

People tell me all the time, "Oh, I was just in Pittsburgh and I had no idea, what an amazing city." Every time I go there, I still get chills every time I go through the Fort Pitt Tunnel and I come out…I can only imagine coming through there for the first time for someone who's never seen it, it's amazing. Then there's the sheer panic trying to figure out which of the twelve freeway signs they are supposed understand and follow within two seconds while they're looking at the skyline then saying, "Holy shit, where am I supposed to go?!"

In Pittsburgh you're all in it together…I don't see that in other cities. In a way, Pittsburgh is your family, and that's why people are so proud of it and want to talk about it like you want to talk about your kids or your parents or your cousins because you love them so much. I don't see it in other cities… maybe Chicago a little bit…but Pittsburgh just has these values to be nice to people; these are the people that made Pittsburgh great, that's a tradition that you have to carry on. It's passed down…you gotta know you can put a chair outside and save your parking spot. It's those things that aren't written down anywhere—they're instilled and passed down…you gotta root for the Steelers and badmouth the Browns for the rest of your life. The unwritten rules of Pittsburgh: be nice to strangers and make sure anyone that comes into town you have to take them to Primanti's and Mount Washington.

ROGER HUMPHRIES

Born into a family of ten children, Roger Humphries began playing drums at age four and went professional at age fourteen. He led an ensemble at Carnegie Hall at age sixteen. In the early the 1960s, he began touring with jazz musicians, including one of his more prominent gigs in a trio with Stanley Turrentine and Shirley Scott.

I have never known life without music, it's roots. I'm the youngest one of ten, and as a kid I always had music in the house and I've had support from my whole family about my music.

Between my Uncle Fatman Frank Humphries, who played with Tab Smith; my Uncle Hildred, who played the saxophone; and musically inclined older brothers Lawrence and Norman, I was surrounded by music growing up. I began playing the drums at the age of four when Norman introduced me to the instrument, which was a natural thing for me. I was imitating him, and I guess to be honest with you, the drums chose me. I got in love with it, and I've been playing ever since that early age.

Courtesy BNY Mellon Jazz.

I grew up around musicians, so the big names like Ray Charles didn't faze me. At that age, I didn't really think about it because it was kind of a natural thing to be around all of the heavyweights, the older musicians, because of my brothers and two older uncles.

As a teenager, I frequented the Hurricane Club and the Crawford Grill, two former jazz hotspots in the Hill District. It was at the Crawford Grill that, among others, where I met Art Blakey and Max Roach, two prolific drummers that I considers my mentors. The Crawford Grill was so much of a learning place for me because they took me when I was a kid.

At fourteen, I began my professional jazz career and went on to work with musicians such as Stanley Turrentine and Shirley Scott, Ray Charles, Horace Silver, James Moody, Benny Green and many more. I was inspired by the musicians that came to Pittsburgh, and that the most important lesson I learned was to pass on the jazz tradition. They'd come to the Crawford Grill, and I would sit up there and watch them play; then they would have me get up on the bandstand and make me play.

That's the relationship you should have with students…they can't just watch you. You gotta put them on the field to see if they can handle it by themselves. This is why I'm fortunate to be in Pittsburgh. The students that I teach, I tell them, "You can't just take a lesson from me. You've gotta apply it with the band. How else are you going to learn?" That's how I learned.

I left in 1962 to pursue my music career. I joined the Horace Silver Quintet, toured Europe with the band twice and played at the Monterey Jazz Festival, and cultivated my place in the world of jazz by playing with the likes of Grant Green and Ray Charles. I fondly remember Ray as a kind man and excellent chess player. Growing up in the music world, you think you'd never get the chance to play with him, but I did.

I consider my time on the road time well spent. What drew me back to Pittsburgh was my family. I grew up in a large family, and to me, family is very important because you can't go back and relive something that you wanted to do. Music is very important in life, but I wanted to take the vibe that I got in New York back to Pittsburgh.

When I returned to Pittsburgh in 1969, I continued to find joy in performing, but my life as a musician took a different tune…I became a teacher at Pittsburgh Creative and Performing Arts School and the University of Pittsburgh. My school with music was always studying at the nightclub with other musicians, and I didn't know if I'd be capable at first. But I figured out I had something to share with the students, and I enjoyed seeing them make progress and who they became in the music world. Art and Max, when I was coming up at the Crawford Grill, it was all about passing it on, and I always had that feeling because they were always passing it on to me, letting me sit in and play. I always wanted to do jam sessions the same way because maybe nobody else thought this kid could play, but if you gave him a chance you see that he had talent and was something that he wanted to do. So I always had that passion for the musicians.

The Crawford Grill to me was like a family. I knew Mr. Robinson, Buzzy Robinson, and they were always very warm to me when I came into the place. You would see everybody, everybody you could think of they all came to the Crawford Grill. It was another school for me.

Pittsburgh is one of a kind. You can do the research of how many musicians came out of Pittsburgh…it is crazy, man. It's a spirit to me. Pittsburgh just has a certain spirit that you can't find in other places because of the way we came up like we did with all of the musicians here. I understand what they meant about the crossroads of the United States when it came to the music. People would come from New York City, and from Pittsburgh they would go on to Chicago. It was beautiful, man, and for me to grow up here, live on the North Side, and the Crawford Grill and other places that weren't that far. The Hurricane, me and Georgie Benson we were kids, young people, we played together. It's been a wonderful place for me.

I have no plans to slow down. I'm looking forward to benefits, singing commitments with friends and my annual Jazz on the River Boat Ride. My plans for the future are to try to continue sharing the music and passing on the help that was given to me. There's nothing like music. No matter what field you get into, you can separate yourself from the world, just you and your music.

TOM SAVINI

Actor/SFX wizard/stuntman/director Tom Savini was inspired by the film Man of a Thousand Faces *in 1957 and became fascinated with the magic and illusion of film. He spent his youth in his room creating characters by tirelessly practicing makeup. He acquired a remarkable cult following among film fans, primarily due to his groundbreaking SFX in the "splatter movie" explosion of the early 1980s.*

Everything I've done started because of one movie and how I was influenced by my father, my four brothers and sister, and I did it all while living here in Pittsburgh. I've never lost my sense of home because I'm still here.

When I was growing up, my dad could do anything. He was a carpenter, a plumber, an electrician, a bricklayer, a shoemaker and many, many more things, all while working full time at the steel mill. I imagine he was so good at many things because being an immigrant he had to be good at many things to survive. I grew up thinking you're supposed to do many things well. Before I was born, my mother had five children—four brothers and my sister—there's thirteen years between me and my sister and she's the youngest of that group, so I had four fathers, four big influences on my life.

Henry was the oldest and he was the smart guy…he had books all over the place. Music, art, he was a painter, a tattoo artist and a sculptor. He was studying to be a mortician, so as a kid I would see him sculpting a big Egyptian head, I think he was practicing restorative makeup. He was a big artistic influence and intellectual influence. The next brother was Sullivan, and he influenced me as far as physical fitness goes. He was a big muscular guy, was in the Korean War. Then there was Joe…Joe was a terrific dancer, and when he danced the floor would clear and everybody would watch

Courtesy YouTube.

him. And he had a great sense of humor…he would put wigs on and false teeth just to make us laugh. And after him was Tony, the only brother that stuck around, the only brother who lived in the house with me growing up. I remember sitting around and watching Hal Holbrook doing Mark Twain. I was interested in Mark Twain because Dick Smith had done Hal Holbrook's makeup, so he was a big influence because he was the guy who was into me being into makeup.

When I was a kid, the Sunday paper was important because of the comics. You had these great big color comics. I would sit there and watch my sister with a sketchbook and colored pencils. By the end of the day, she had copied in color pencil the Sunday comics, and you couldn't tell the difference between what she was doing and the Sunday comics. It was brilliant, and that gave me the appreciation of being able to sit there with a blank page and create something.

My mother was a huge influence on me.…I mean I adored her. She's been gone more than forty years now, and every now and then it will come back to me how important she was in my life. She was the one who would let me stay up all night to watch horror movies after my dad would make me go up to bed. My mother would let me sneak back down and watch horror movies on the black-and-white TV when I was a kid because she knew how much I loved horror movies. I would be up in my room and would make myself up to be Zachary, or some kind of fuzzy, green werewolf, and come down the stairs as quietly as I could and stand behind her while she was watching television and just wait for her to turn and make her scream. I feel bad sometimes of how bad I used to scare her, but when I wanted to go to the movies I always had enough money and my mother would take me. I remember my mother taking me to see Rodan and Godzilla movies at the Plaza Theater up the street.

I spent my childhood at the Plaza movie theater in Bloomfield. I saw the *Creature from the Black Lagoon* when it opened here in 1954. Now it's a corporate coffeehouse. It was a travesty when it closed about five years ago.…It opened in 1917, and I was a kid going there in the '50s, '60s and '70s even until the '90s. [*From*] *Dusk Till Dawn* played here when it opened, but now it's gone—another house of magic is gone.

Watching television when I was a kid, *Father Knows Best* and all of these sitcoms, I always wondered why my life was never like that. Thinking back on it, we were poor, we had nothing. Thank God the movies were only twenty-five cents because movies were my escape into other worlds, other families. The various genres…I loved westerns, but I really loved horror movies. I saw a movie called *Man of a Thousand Faces* at the Plaza Theater when I was twelve years old, and I flipped out.

Before seeing *Man of a Thousand Faces*, I thought the characters were real, that Frankenstein was real, the Wolf Man, the Creature from the Black Lagoon....I thought they were real [and] that's why they scared me so much, I was so afraid of them. But *Man of a Thousand Faces* showed me that somebody creates the monsters. But that movie was the catalyst, was the springboard for me pursuing the career that I have chosen. From that day on, I was reading about makeup. With the launch in 1958 of the magazine *Famous Monsters of Filmland*, I was twelve and I would gather all of my friends around me, and we would leaf through the pages of famous monsters and it was like watching *Indiana Jones*—it was spectacular, it was a big thrill to see this magazine. And, of course, I would try to make them up like one of the characters we had seen in the magazine. So that was great fun, except they would go home with cut throats and half their hair burned off—not really but with makeup.

I was like the gang leader, the monster guy, and I would shine shoes in the neighborhood to buy a mask or makeup. I still collect masks from all over the world. So that's basically my childhood until the age of fourteen. I became Dracula as part of traveling show, and they paid in chocolate milk shakes and silver dollars.

The big deal at the time was Saturday Night…Saturday night *Chiller Theatre* with Bill Cardille or Chilly Billy Cardilly would host and interrupt in the commercial spaces horror movies. You looked forward to Saturday Night and watching those horror movies on Chiller Theater; that's where you were every Saturday night…you were guaranteed to be home watching Chilly Billy Cardilly on *Chiller Theatre*.

I've worked in Hong Kong, I've worked in South Africa. I've been everywhere, but I always come home to Bloomfield and Pittsburgh. I think I live a charmed life here in Bloomfield and in Pittsburgh.

EDUCATION

KEN GORMLEY

Kenneth Gerald Gormley is an American lawyer, academic and author who is the thirteenth president of Duquesne University. He is a former dean and a tenured professor of constitutional law at the Thomas R. Kline School of Law of Duquesne University. His novel, The Heiress of Pittsburgh *(2021), has received widespread acclaim for capturing the essence of his hometown.*

I grew up on the border of Edgewood and Swissvale, so my home was technically in Edgewood, right across from the entrance to Union Switch & Signal. We went to school at St. Anselm's in Swissvale, so although summers were more focused on Koenig Field in Edgewood, I spent most of my time growing up in Swissvale. It was a true working-class town. I went to bed at night and would hear the railroad cars banging against each other at the Union Switch. When you closed your eyes and listened, you could hear the barge whistles drifting up from the river. It was a very special place to be. Ultimately, when I got married, I liked to say that "Forest Hills is where people from Swissvale went when they made it." That's where we ended up. My wife came from New Jersey, and I pointed out to her (when we bought our house) that we at least managed to get ten minutes away from where I grew up, so that was a victory.

There were many special things about these little neighborhoods. When I went off to law school at Harvard, it became even clearer that I wanted nothing more than to return home and contribute something where I had grown up. It had left a massive impression on me. One of my law school roommates is now Senator Mark Warner of Virginia, who just hosted a book party for me in Washington when my novel, *The Heiress of Pittsburgh*, was released; there were people from Harvard, people from Pittsburgh, people from all over the country. Warner stood up and said, "This book is no surprise—the whole time we were together all this guy talked about was how Pittsburgh was the greatest place in the world." I grabbed the microphone and interjected, "Well, I was *right!*"

Pittsburgh is more than just a place that you're from or a place where you happen to hang your hat. It's a real family, a sort of community, and the people I grew up with in Edgewood and Swissvale are still among my very best friends in life. My (recently retired) assistant at Duquesne, Peggy Eiseman, I've known since kindergarten. We all went to St. Anselm's grade school and high school together. There's an element of trust and knowing there's no hidden agenda in anything you do or say. That makes it special and different from relationships I've had with almost anyone else except my family and my closest friends from Harvard Law School. It's a precious thing. I suspect it does exist in some other parts of the country, but for a larger city I'm not sure there is anything quite like what we have in the Burgh.

I had the happiest childhood a person could ever have. A lot of it was because there were such close-knit neighborhoods. We went from house to house, street to street playing kickball, "release" and shooting hoops. It was just a moving adventure every day. Koenig Field in the summers was a magical place; there was badminton, and one family had a monkey that they would bring to the park a couple times a summer. Every year the monkey would escape and go up this giant tree, and they would have to bring the

Courtesy Duquesne University.

Edgewood Fire Department to rescue it, so there was always plenty of excitement there. There was a balloon derby where you would let balloons go with postcards to see whose went the farthest, and a few would end up in distant places like Ohio and New Jersey. And there was a lot of exploring that went on. I knew every inch of the woods. I could still walk through the woods in Edgewood, Swissvale, Frick Park and know every inch of those places. We rode our bikes through Frick Park and into the slag dump trails, which were not made for bicycles, but we figured out how to navigate them. It was a true adventure, but there were a lot of people in it with you, looking out for you and making sure that everything was okay.

One of the things about my childhood that was uniquely Pittsburgh, even though I didn't think of it that way at the time, was being a *Post-Gazette* paperboy. That was a magical time to be up at 5:30 in the morning. It was quiet and you would deliver papers to the little houses, and the lights would blink on, and you would go into back alleys and cut through yards. Many of the people were just fabulous—I remember one older Slovak lady who would come out on Christmas Day when I was delivering the paper with a hot nutroll for me that she had just baked as my Christmas gift. Speaking of Pittsburgh delicacies, I worked at Isaly's in Regent Square, so I made skyscraper ice cream cones and probably ate as many as I served to customers. That was an iconic place, and I always point out—when I see these Pittsburghese books that talk about "chipped-chopped ham"—that the sign on the window may have said Isaly's "chipped-chopped ham," but no self-respecting Pittsburgher would ever call it "chipped-chopped ham." They would say, "Give me a pound a' chipped ham!"

There were lots of very special experiences as a kid in Pittsburgh that I look back on now and realize they were distinctly Pittsburgh, even though I didn't know it at the time.

It's hard to capture what make a place so special, but I've thought about it a lot in pondering what makes Pittsburgh Pittsburgh. The thing that jumps out at me is the trustworthiness, the integrity that people had—people would do anything to help others, even if they didn't have much themselves. A lot of the people I grew up with, most of them worked in the mills. They worked at the Union Switch or Edgar Thompson mills, so these were not people who were highly educated in terms of formal education but they were amazingly talented people who could make incredible things with their hands. The values that they had of looking out for each other—which really came from looking out for each other at the mills—extended into their families and communities. It was always about caring about others and trying to do things that would make life better for everyone. There was an honor and pride in doing that.

It underlines what we sense is so special about Pittsburgh, even though it defies a simple written definition. I had a job offer at a law firm in Hawaii, an offer to teach at the University of Miami, and in each case I said, "Well, it just isn't Pittsburgh." So I turned them down. I didn't know exactly what I wanted to do in terms of a specific career, but I knew I wanted to make a contribution to this place that had done so much for me.

In my family, we never went out to eat and we never went on vacations except to visit family. Every nickel was saved by my mom and dad for education. For my graduation from Harvard Law School, my mom and dad and my little sister arrived in Boston in the Dodge Dart after making the voyage all the way up there. It was such a happy moment to see them in the crowd; it was the first time they'd been to Harvard during my three years there. We reached this moment when all my classmates were going off to dinner at these fancy restaurants, and mom and dad said, "We'll take to you to dinner. Where would you like to go?" That was the first time in my life that they'd offered to go out to eat—so I picked Charlie's Beef & Beer when everyone else was going to expensive restaurants. I figured hamburgers at Charlie's Beef & Beer was a modest selection, and I knew they'd feel comfortable there. So we were having hamburgers and a plate of fries and in walked a lady with sunglasses and another young lady accompanied by guys with dark jackets on. It turned out to be Jackie Kennedy Onassis and Caroline Kennedy, who had graduated from Harvard College that same day. Apparently the Secret Service and the Kennedys had decided they'd better avoid the high-end places where they'd be recognized, so they came to Charlie's Beef & Beer. I ended up having the best spot of all for my graduation dinner. And I felt on top of the world because I had conquered the challenge of Harvard Law School, but I was now going home.

A few years later, when I met my wife, Laura, who is from New Jersey, I had to break the news to her that "I love you dear. I'll do anything for you except move away from Pittsburgh!" So I always say that she gave me that one—but she's won all the other family decisions since then. I just couldn't see myself anywhere else. It was a part of who I was, and it was tied so closely to what I wanted to do in my life, which involved doing something for these special people I had grown up with.

Now, as president of Duquesne University, it's one of the reasons I feel that I have the greatest job in the world. Not only did I grow up with Catholic education being important, but Duquesne represents precisely the rich Pittsburgh heritage that means so much to me. In the late 1800s and into the 1900s, people of many different nationalities were coming to Duquesne, and the Spiritan priests were helping them to lift themselves up through education because they were marginalized, they were immigrants. They were coming here to work in the factories and didn't have a lot of material things. Education was the key to a better, more rewarding life and a pathway to helping others achieve the same. For me, carrying on that tradition is one of the greatest honors of this job. I always say that Duquesne University helped to build Pittsburgh, and it's true. Now this work is a continuation, an extension, of all of the wonderful qualities that I was lucky enough to absorb as a young person growing up in Swissvale and Edgewood. Preserving it for future generations, including my own kids and grandkids, is the greatest privilege imaginable.

SAMUEL HAZO

Spanning six decades and circling the globe, author Samuel Hazo's oeuvre includes poetry, fiction, drama, essays and various works of translation. He has published more than fifty books. As founder and director of the International Poetry Forum from 1966 until 2009, Dr. Hazo hosted more than eight hundred distinguished poets and performers from around the world, establishing Pittsburgh as a cultural and artistic nerve center.

I grew up in Squirrel Hill. We lived on Murray Hill Avenue originally and then Wilkins Avenue and finally moved into what was then East Liberty, on Shady Avenue, but I've lived in Upper St. Clair now for sixty-three years. And basically my memories of Pittsburgh are of the time when it was a smoky city. The mills were thriving. There were mornings I would walk from Shady Avenue to Central Catholic High School, and if I held my hand in front of my face, I couldn't see my fingers. That's how bad the smog was.

My love of writing started in college. I had some very good teachers there. I began writing poems and short stories, and when I was in the Marine Corps, I began writing there just to survive and continued after that for the same reason....I write the way I breathe, the same necessity. I can't will myself to write, I have to be compelled, inspired or influenced to write something. That's the only way I've worked over the years, and the medium chooses itself.

I went to Notre Dame on a scholarship from Dr. Leo O'Donnell here in Pittsburgh, a wonderful man who always supported a student at Notre Dame because he was an alumnus. He interviewed about three or four of us from Central Catholic, and he called me the next day and said, "How would you like to attend Notre Dame?" Within a month, I found myself at the end of June on a train to South Bend, Indiana. I owe Notre Dame so much because

*Courtesy Bob Donaldson/*Post-Gazette.

I was introduced there to what education really was. It was not getting a degree; it was learning in the real sense of the word. I had so many inspiring teachers there, and I still credit them.

Growing up, the course of my life was determined by my upbringing. Education was very important to my mother, and my mother's parents were interested in song and poetry. As she grew, my mother became interested in those things too, as did my Aunt Katherine, who raised my brother and me after our mother died. In our home, the grown-ups would also speak rather poetically, at times in Arabic, a language that I did not understand. But when I listened, even as a small child, I know that I was hearing thoughts and feelings expressed in a mode of speech that was above the normal.

Pittsburgh is really the only place where I feel at home, and unless you have a sense of place, you can't really write anything that is worth anything. Some years ago, Pittsburgh was named the "Most Livable City in America." Rand McNally touted that, and a lot of the writers came from New York to write about it. Well, I was reading their stories, and I didn't recognize the city in anything they wrote. So I wrote an essay that was published in *Carnegie Magazine*, and over the years that essay became a book, *The Pittsburgh That Stays Within You*. Last year I was told it won the creative nonfiction award from the Independent Press Association.

As I said, at an early age and later in college, I came to the conclusion that poetry was one medium where you could and should express feelings accurately. I still believe in that. You can't do it in prose, but poetry can bear it. Initially, I was inclined to be a lawyer. Thank God I decided against it. But I decided to major in English and had a teacher named Frank O'Malley, who introduced me to not only English but to American and continental literature as well, the latter, which focusing on literary movements such as humanism, existentialism and absurdity in modern European literature.

While teaching at Duquesne University, I invited a poet, W.H. Auden, to visit the school, and in introducing him, I said it would be wonderful if poets could read their or say their poems to the public at large and not just to students and teachers. There was a fellow named Ted Hazlett who called me the next day and said, "I like your idea, Let's try that in Pittsburgh for a year." I said, "Mr. Hazlett I wouldn't touch it for a year; it will take a year to get our name in the phone book." He said, "All right, five years renewable annually." So we turned away three hundred people in the rain at the first reading of the International Poetry Forum by Archibald MacLeish. Then Yevgeny Yevtushenko came about a month later. We filled Carnegie Music Hall, and it has continued since then. It's about six hundred to seven hundred poets have come to Pittsburgh from thirty-eight different countries plus the United States. I'm very proud of what we did, which was something that punctuated the personality of the world in the city, and I'm grateful to have had the chance to have done it.

I like to think that we brought something very different to the city of Pittsburgh, and a lot of people have felt the same. The International Poetry Forum was unique in the world. There's nothing like it that exists where people come and pay to hear poets say their poems. Those poets all had different reactions to the city. MacLeish said openly the first time he was here, "This may seem unimportant to many people in the world, but it will be important." And Yevtushenko said, "I found in Pittsburgh what I looked for when I came to America." We got comments like that over forty-three years.

We were fortunate to have Paul Mellon back the Poetry Forum. It was his foundation that Ted Hazlett represented here in Pittsburgh. After about ten years, he wrote me a letter....It was a very simple thing...he said, "Dear Sam, poetry is alive at 785 Summerville Drive. Yours truly, Paul Mellon." He was a wonderful man; he was totally indifferent to money. But for anything to work, it takes money and an idea. Neither can work alone. A good idea needs resources.

I'm now ninety-four, and the only way to explain my good fortune is to say that I've been lucky. In the Hazo family, we have only one rule for living: No matter what you do, make sure you love to do it. In other words, choose what you love to do, no matter what it takes, and there's no way you'll end up miserable. Maybe you'll have it hard here and there, but eventually, things will work out for the best.

EVAN WOLFSON

Evan Wolfson is an internationally recognized civil rights lawyer and strategist. He founded and led Freedom to Marry, the campaign that won marriage equality in the United States, and is widely considered the architect of the movement that led to nationwide victory in 2015. In 1983, Wolfson wrote his Harvard Law School thesis on gay people and the freedom to marry. During the 1990s, he served as co-counsel in the historic Hawaii marriage case that launched the ongoing global movement for the freedom to marry and has participated in numerous gay rights and HIV/AIDS cases. Wolfson earned a BA in history from Yale College in 1978; served as a Peace Corps volunteer in a village in Togo, West Africa; and wrote the book Why Marriage Matters: America, Equality, and Gay People's Right to Marry, *published by Simon & Schuster in July 2004. In 2012, he was inducted into the Taylor Allderdice Hall of Fame.*

I was born and lived in Brooklyn for my first year and a half, then my parents moved to Pittsburgh and I lived there, except for a short stint in Texas during my dad's service in the army, until I went to college.

My formative childhood years were, thus, definitely Pittsburgh. I always, as a kid, thought of myself as a New Yorker living in Pittsburgh. As I get older and have lived a vast majority of my life in New York though, I'm very aware that I am also a Pittsburgher. I have the Pittsburgh roots and feel very appreciative of what I had in Pittsburgh during my life there with my family, the friendships and the perspective that Pittsburgh adds to my life as a New Yorker. Even after returning to New York City, I continued going back to Pittsburgh to visit my parents, my grandmother, my siblings and, eventually, my niece and nephews, and still visit frequently.

I consider both New York City and Pittsburgh as my hometowns. The quality of Pittsburgh that most resonates for me is the idea of community. Growing up with a loving community in warm and welcoming Pittsburgh, I always believed that we could all dream of love and inclusion. There is this very strong feeling of living in a manageable community, a sense of community and a consciousness of a city of communities in Pittsburgh. That's what I took from Pittsburgh that might have been different had I grown up in New York.

Courtesy Freedom to Marry.

Pittsburgh was a steel town when I was growing up, but my family didn't have a direct connection to the steel industry and the blue-collar world, although I was obviously aware of it. We would drive past steel mills, but that wasn't my Pittsburgh in a sense. My Pittsburgh was much more shaped by growing up in Squirrel Hill and being part of the Jewish community, not in an intense religious way but much more in a cultural, familial and even geographic way. If you take all of those elements of Pittsburgh, a city of communities, a city very conscious of community, the value of community, that's what has left a bigger imprint on me and my family.

I was very lucky to have grown up in a very loving and close family who, like many families, may have gotten on each other's nerves and bickered but always felt deep love and very connected in each other's lives. My parents always put the kids first and drummed into us the importance of our connection as siblings and identity as a family.

I also benefited from having great schools like Linden and Allderdice and friendships that I still have from those days. My elementary school and high school friendships continue to this day. Also the terrific education that I received was an important influence. I'm still in touch through Facebook with Bill Fisher, the legendary principal, who came in to Allderdice back when I was a student there. He's still going strong in his nineties, and I enjoy chiming in on his and high school friends' Facebook pages to this day.

The Squirrel Hill neighborhood enabled us to be part of this larger circle that existed within the bigger world of Pittsburgh, how important those formative experiences are and those friendships are. I am constantly made aware of how important and how lucky I was growing up where I did and having all that I had.

One other thing I acquired in Squirrel Hill and still have very much to this day is a love of street life. Today, it is being able to go out of my New York apartment and be in the middle of it, go to stores, go to restaurants, be surrounded by activity and people, as opposed to a more "driving"-centered life that many people have. We had Forbes and Murray and the ability to walk. In my day, we walked to school even as a kid living on Forbes Avenue. We would walk to Wightman, my first elementary school. At six, seven and eight, it seemed like an immeasurably long walk, and I doubt many kids growing up in cities today would be allowed to do that walk, but my sister and I were sent off every day. That definitely put an imprint on me, and walking is part of loving and living in New York, and my pleasure in cities where I can just tumble out and be in the middle of things.

I was the kind of kid who was always told at an early age that I should be a lawyer. I had a passion for history and politics and always wanted to be involved in something that would make history and make a difference. When I think of my childhood in Pittsburgh, I was very verbal, liked to argue, and I always wanted to accomplish something, so law, politics and government were the natural avenues that appealed to me right from an early age. From those passions, I always assumed that I would go to law school. I enjoyed watching TV shows about law and lawyers, but being a lawyer was not the end of itself. To me, it was the means to be involved in politics, government, activism, making a difference.

From childhood on, that's what I wanted. I walked around the neighborhood collecting money for Israel during the Six-Day War because I was motivated to make a difference and contribute there. This came out of me, but my parents supported it. It happened because I would be reading the news—even wanting to get a subscription to the *New York Times*.

Pittsburgh was a big city, bigger in my day, but has a small-town feel to it that makes it more manageable and understandable. Pittsburgh was small enough that you felt like you could walk in, you could see it, you could watch government, you could know businesses, you could tour the Heinz factory. As a kid, I even got in to interview the mayor for our school paper. Experiences like that helped me frame how I saw the world as a kid and allowed me to put images to what I was reading about. That was part of Pittsburgh's contribution to the way I see the world now as a New Yorker, as a traveler, as someone who has worked nationally and internationally…I still have the Pittsburgh community-scale sensibility that helps me manage that world.

We lived two and a half blocks away from Tree of Life, which became our family synagogue. I was bar mitzvahed at Tree of Life. I went to Hebrew school and Sunday school at Tree of Life for years and years during my childhood, so, of course, like everyone, but with the particular intensity of watching yet another gun rampage on TV thinking, "That's mine," I felt the horror of the attack there. And then felt pride in how the community and city responded.

Every time I go back to visit every couple of months, driving past Tree of Life, I feel deeply moved and touched by both the memories of what it meant to all of us and what it represents for the work we need to do to get our country to a better place. Alongside my childhood memories, the influence of Pittsburgh now includes a call to action to get American democracy back on track.

BROADCAST

AMANDA BALIONIS RENNER

Amanda Balionis Renner is a popular American sports journalist on CBS for golf, the NFL and college football. Her charm and humor have quickly won the hearts of viewers and professional sports personalities alike. When not on the golf course, she is focused on her campaigns for Puppies & Golf, K9s for Warriors and Girls n' Golf that are supported by Calloway Golf.

When I look back at my childhood in Mount Lebanon, I think they are some of my favorite memories, not with just my mom and dad but my whole family. Watching Steelers games on my grandmother's couch with my cousins all together. It was always the moments when everyone was the happiest, having fun together, a true distraction from the real world, especially when you're born in Pittsburgh you are just born with football in your blood. It's impossible not to love the Steelers, not to root for them, and it's impossible to not appreciate the passion the entire city has.

I have had the opportunity to work with the Steelers during this past off season, and every Uber and cab had a Terrible Towel on their front dash. Even when it's not football season, you know you're going to spot one in every five people walking down the street in a Steelers jersey or a Dan Marino jersey from high school.

It's just such a passionate city, and it totally trickled down where everything stops on Steelers Sundays. Dinner was around the TV watching games, or we were inviting friends over for the one o'clock games and you

Courtesy Stephen Denton.

had to leave if you weren't a Steelers fan. It was always something that we loved to do as a family, and again those memories are full of fun and happiness, and being on the same team while ignoring all of the other stuff going on in our lives. Really special memories that encouraged me to pursue that as a profession. If I can find this much joy and get paid for it and bring that much joy to others by reporting on these games, why wouldn't I do that? That's the genesis of it all for me.

I majored in broadcast journalism at Hofstra University, and when I graduated, I started out on the sidelines in the New York area. In 2011, I interviewed for a digital position with PGATour.com. I thought it was such a great opportunity to cover professional sports. The PGA Tour really trained me from day one to learn the game of golf, to live it and breathe it.

My whole family are golf fanatics. My grandparents met on a golf course. My parents play virtually every day, so I grew up around the game. I took lessons at a golf course where I grew up, when I was little, probably like eight or nine years old. I played junior golf for a few years, and even though I stopped playing junior golf around thirteen years old, I was still going out with my parents weekly to play a little loop around my house.

I'll be honest, pretty much every time that Jim Nantz says my name as part of the crew at the top of the broadcast, I'll still giggle. And every time he throws it down to me, I'm thinking in my head, "Oh my gosh, Jim Nantz is throwing it down to me." And I wonder if one of these times I'm just gonna be laughing once I'm on.

At Oakmont in 2016, being from Pittsburgh, being there with my family was amazing. But Callaway allowed me to run with this idea of doing trick shots at Heinz Field with Jim Furyk. Jim said, "All right, I'll do it. But you have to make it cool." So I asked myself how I could make it cool. I reached out to Burt Lauten, who is the communications director for the Steelers, actually through Twitter, and he said, "Sure, how about I get Ben Roethlisberger?" We called Jim, and he said, "Yeah let's do it." So I spent my thirtieth birthday during the U.S. Open at Heinz Field in my hometown watching Jim Furyk and Ben Roethlisberger hit chip shots at the home of the Steelers. It literally couldn't have been any better for me.

I loved Three Rivers Stadium and loved going to games there. It's where I fell in love with football and also where I learned all of my swear words.

I can tell you every one of my favorite Steelers bars in every city that I've lived. It's bringing people together even when you have nothing else in common; you know when you show up at a Steelers bar on a Sunday you know you're going to have an amazing time with passionate, smart football fans. That's just what it is. I had the chance to cover a Steelers-Cardinals game in Arizona, and it felt like a Steelers home game. It was 75 percent Steelers fans, and it just reminded me of why I do this. It's a special, fun environment and group of people.

It's interesting when you talk about how the city had to fight through tough times. I was raised by two Pittsburgh parents who grew up in Pittsburgh; their parents grew up in Pittsburgh, and we go back. This idea of work hard and reinvent yourself when you need to was a constant theme in my life and teaching lessons from my parents. My grandfather worked in the steel mill, making pretty good money, when he was scouted by Wake Forest, who asked him to go play football and baseball and he said, "No, I'm okay. I'm going to stay in the steel mill." His boss called him in and fired him on the spot and said, "You're out of here. You have to go to Wake Forest and pursue an education."

But these gritty hardworking families that didn't have much but always figured it out—those lessons absolutely trickle down generationally. I think that's a large part of who I am today. I still have notes from my mom that she would leave me on my bathroom mirror to continue to pursue the dreams that you have. I can't imagine that messaging would have been the same if we weren't all touched by Pittsburgh in that way.

BOB POMPEANI

A sports anchor for KDKA News, Bob Pompeani began his career at KDKA Television in 1982, but his experience with hometown sports goes beyond the forty-plus years he's worked at the station. Growing up in an area deep in sports traditions, Pompeani has seen all of the biggest high school rivalries as well as met players and coaches who've gone on to make sports history.

I was always fixated on sports. I loved sports, I always have. I'm a big believer that anyone who gets into anything in life has to be passionate about it. If not, you're wasting your time, probably.

I played baseball at Hopewell High School, I played golf…golf was my passion. I worked hard at it. My father was a member at Aliquippa Country Club, which is now called Beaver Lakes. My brother and I both played a lot, we got into it, we caddied, we were just very much enthralled with golf. I kind of emerged as the number one guy on the Hopewell golf team. I was looking for a golf scholarship.

When I was seventeen, though, I could tell there was something wrong with my heartbeat; it became rather sporadic, and I was noticing it and I told my parents. Six months earlier, I had a cold or a viral infection, and I didn't think anything of it, but it turned out to be Strep throat. What maybe most people don't realize is that as a teenager, Strep throat can do some damage to your heart valve. It does attack, and it goes specifically to heart valves, which happened to me and I had no idea. I went in to get it checked, and they said I had a heart murmur at first. And the more they examined me it turned out to be a manic heart disease caused by Strep throat that affected my aortic valve and my mitral valve. I had the first of two open-heart surgeries when I was seventeen and a half, and that surgery back then was very different than today. They had to essentially crack your sternum, really cut you in half to get to your heart, and replace the valves. They took my heart out of my chest, made the repairs and brought it back in.

As a young aspiring golfer, that was not very good news since the sternum is a big part of your golf swing, so I knew that was going to be a problem. It was a down time in my life; golf was my passion, and I couldn't play competitively again. My father always told me, "You love sports"—and we did, we always watched and talked about it—"why don't you find something to do in sports? You have a good voice, maybe you can get into this."

It took me a while to get over it. Like normal, there was a "why me" period, and maybe it was God's way of saying, "You're not going to be that good anyway, so I'm doing you a favor, pal." I started to dig in doing things at Hopewell High School…public address, some public speaking. There was a guy named Bill Fontana, he used to be the general manager at WMBA Radio in Ambridge. I had never met him, but I knew where he lived so I started leaving donuts at his doorstep every night—I worked at Bambino's

Courtesy Becky Thurner Braddock.

Donuts in Sewickley—and I would make donuts and pizza. I said I had to get to know this guy somehow, someway, and I left a little note that said, "I live a couple of houses up with my dad, mom and my brother and I would like to get to know you." I kept bringing donuts. I was pretty persistent about that. Finally I got to meet him, and I got an opportunity to do some radio at the local level. From there, I worked at it best I could, met people, all the things you would try to do who was aspiring to get into the sports field.

Meeting and knowing people in Pittsburgh gave me my start. Bill Fontana was a big help, then people at WMBA and WBVP in Beaver Falls. Guy Junker and I got started doing high school football play-by-play and color every Friday night, so we worked together quite a bit. I've had many that I have admired over the years: Bob Smizik, Gene Collier—the guys I used to work with. And Myron Cope…I got to know him, and he was very helpful for me when I first started. I'm just amazed how fortunate we are to have these great people, like Greg Brown, who I went to Point Park University with, and he's now the play-by-play guy for the Pittsburgh Pirates…Mike Lange and Bill Hillgrove were very helpful too. I could just go on and on.

In Pittsburgh, family and community are both important, but it starts at home. My parents were the most supportive parents, no matter what I wanted to do. With golf it was all in, they drove me to golf tournaments, whatever it took. My mother was my biggest fan, and I had to tell her to be more objective with me at times—you don't always have to think I'm the best. My father would offer some criticisms when necessary, and I wanted it—tell me what you really think. I have never met a better man than my father. Anyone who has gone through a good situation with their parents would say that, and it's how it should be, but your role models should be the people who know you, raised you, instilled the values that you have. My mom and dad did that so well, and it has enabled me to do that with my kids too. You learn from stuff you see in your own family, and so it's like a tradition of how you treat people, how you deal with family and all of the issues that come with it.

Traditions play such a big part of Pittsburgh. It's been all about covering communities and how communities came together. I learned early on at Hopewell High School how meaningful it was to be at these sporting events and the support you got from people—people you can count on. You may want a different perspective from people you can trust not named your parents. I had a lot of those kind of friends and learned how people cared for you. I'm glad I grew up when I grew up.

I look forward to interactions with people, and I respond to people who respond to me. Pittsburghers love sports, and for me it's fun, like a toy department at a store where I don't have to worry about the hardcore stuff. I think the people here are very special. They're very easy to deal with. A lot of people travel to cities where people won't give you the time of day. One thing I know about Pittsburghers is that everyone is willing to talk to you, and if you need help, they're willing to help. My wife will give me a shopping list and she wonders why it took two hours, but I'm in line talking Steelers at the Market District checkout line. I love to engage with people like that, and I believe you have to be involved in your community and help out when you can.

I don't consider myself to be famous. It's my job. I enjoy it. I love meeting people. I consider it an honor when people know what I do and who I am. That means they must like what I do, and so for me, that's a responsibility that I take very seriously…I very much am who I am, and what you see on TV, you'll see the same thing in person.

I'm one of those people who tries to enjoy every minute of my day every day because you never know when it's going to end. I don't want to waste them because once you do, you don't get them back.

ELLIS CANNON

A native and lifelong resident of Western Pennsylvania, Ellis Cannon lived in Midland, Beaver County, through childhood until 1977. A graduate of the University of Pittsburgh and its School of Law, Cannon was a successful Pittsburgh trial lawyer before establishing himself as one of the most respected, professional and engaging multiple-spectrum media personalities. He has been inducted into four Halls of Fame in broadcasting and media, including the esteemed Beaver County Hall of Fame (2010) and Midland Sports Hall of Fame (2019).

Midland's role and impact on me has lasted a lifetime. I learned my parents' expectations early, and how Midland challenged me to meet them. Together, they forged what followed. It was simple: demand excellence of yourself and never apologize for it.

My Midland experience produced life tools—a toolbox of knowledge—providing the best chance to succeed in court, business, media and, most importantly, as a person.

Courtesy Alchetran.

Belief systems were instilled: effort fuels achievement, overachieving could trump talent, failure does not define you and indeed accompanies success, grinding is good, honors demand humility, leadership is earned, respectful is not optional and confidence conquers doubt.

It was here I learned that what is different in us—race, ethnicity, faith and personal orientation—makes us stronger, vibrant and a better people. Embracing diversity in my core took root here.

Those are just some reasons Midland people are different. Family, coaches, neighbors and teachers ensured it. Indeed, these all led to many blessings and enhancement of life experiences.

How to apply those beliefs and tools to the tasks of life came in one form or another from Midland, including serving as our football stadium announcer and our legendary boys' basketball Coach Olkowski honoring me at fifteen through graduation with roles as the team scorekeeper and statistician.

I never wanted to disappoint Coach or the guys. What I received in return established pillars that would underscore and enrich my life. It was from him I learned the power of team sports, that singularity of purpose prevails over differences in skin, that no role was too small and that tenacity and preparation always have a place on any team. He reinforced an essential family tool for success: responsibility comes with accountability, and if you are not accountable, then you are not responsible.

I believe all this happened through God's grace. But I also know if you were raised by family to have high standards and values, if you expected more, you could lead—and win.

Ownership of this story does not belong to me, I'm just part of it. Midland was a place where the good in us came together, when the seeds of sacrifice by those before us were sown and the belief you could change the world one small piece at a time was within us.

Truthfully, I didn't know when the moment to share this would come, but I *knew* it would. I also didn't know my mother—in her ninety-first year—would today celebrate with us what she and my late father, Henry, envisioned those many years ago growing up in Midland.

I also didn't know you would reward the best in us—my wonderful wife, Yvonne—who is the blessing of her sons' lives and a partner whose belief and trust guided and inspired me in times of doubt and despair. Or that my family and their lifelong sacrifices and support would be validated; personal and professional friends who I needed with every step would still be with me today.

Finally, I didn't know Pittsburgh would one day gift my three beloved sons—reinforcing values; underscoring family, tradition, faith and community; and empowering them to accept their own paths and challenges with the same passion, tolerance and tools you provided me.

Then again, I'm a Cannon, I'm from Midland—and they—nor you—should expect anything less.

JIM KRENN

Jim Krenn is a popular American comedian, radio personality, entertainer, speaker and storyteller best known for his work on The DVE Morning Show *on* WDVE Radio *from 1988 to 2011. He has performed with comic legends Jay Leno, Jerry Seinfeld, Howie Mandel, Richard Lewis, Tim Allen, Gilbert Gottfried and Dennis Miller.* Billboard *magazine has named him to its list of "Major Market Personalities of the Year." On five separate occasions, Krenn was voted as one of the "Top Entertainers in the City" by* Pittsburgh *magazine.*

I started playing local clubs during the comedy club era like the Funny Bone and other venues that hosted occasional comedy, like Graffiti. I was working all over the country, too, including New York City, and I had a chance to move to L.A. I got lucky and got on WDVE Radio when they gave me a guest spot where I jived so well with the DJs and producers they hired me. But I always loved this city; it's my hometown. My friends and family are here, there are genuine people here. It's home and I'm so happy that I didn't fall into the temptation of doing different cities in radio and stand-up. Integral to the transition to radio was Gene Romano, vice-president of the station. I was developing different characters, and these voices were perfect for radio and I actually didn't know that. Gene was like a coach, and working at DVE was like having a tremendous coaching staff. They always put me in a position to win.

As I got older, it became more and more clear to me that I wanted to stay the route of being a Pittsburgh guy who still does national things. Nothing is holding me back, but I always wanted to call Pittsburgh home.

Growing up an only child in the Strip District, I lived with my family in an alley located just behind what's the Heinz History Center today. It was a tough place…a neighborhood of immigrant

Courtesy Chris Ithen.

workers, shipping agents, laborers, haulers. Growing up in a neighborhood that included the hustle and bustle of shipping and receiving and the cacophony that accompanies wholesale marketing proved to be an inspiration for later life. Tough as the people were, the community was strong. People were unbelievably nice. We were tight-knit. This is where I found all my characters. I was always the observer. I was always a quiet kid, but the Strip was true Pittsburgh.

My grandmother, mom and dad were big influences in that the family and what you do for others is everything. When I first got on DVE, they had this billboard campaign, and my face is everywhere. On Wednesdays, I used to drive to Shaler to bring my grandmother to South Side bingo, and we had this little ritual that every Wednesday we would also go to Eat'n Park for a fish sandwich. One day, I was on East Street and there was a billboard that was bigger than life, and I said, "Look at that, Grandma." She was really into it, but she actually said something really cool. I was twenty-six and started experiencing being known, and she said, "Grandson, you're really talented, you're going to do great and I'm proud of you, but I want you to remember that you'll always be remembered for what you do for others." And I never forgot that…use your good fortune to help others…and I took that to heart. I started getting involved with Animal Friends, the Epilepsy Foundation and some other great charities; that's helped me learn that enriching others was an important thing to do.

My career was an exponential climb starting with impersonations at the family dinner table, then jokes at school talent shows, then gong shows at bars. It was really working at the time because there weren't a lot of radio people that had a stand-up comedy act. I had notoriety and was able to fill up theaters; that helped build a loyal following. People dream of the kind of support that I was given. The audience on the radio became family, and they carried me. I kind of became their alarm clock, and we got to know each other.

One thing that stuck in my mind, it was a powerful moment of being an entertainer in Pittsburgh. The first year being on the radio, and a woman calls and says, "Hey thanks, Jimmy, for being funny every Thursday at 8:30 a.m. You've been saving me. I get kidney dialysis, and the only thing that gets me through are those bits that you do." That really hit home how important it is to help others.

The one thing about Pittsburgh is that people here can sniff out bullshit. You have to be the real deal. I grew up on 12th Street in the Strip District, which is in the middle of everything. I went to school on the North Side, I had buddies on the South Side, I played baseball in Polish Hill, I was part of the Bloomfield Boxing Club so I was inside all of these neighborhoods. When I was on radio and made references…you had to be there to become an expert on Pittsburgh's people and culture. I started doing the character Stanley P. Kachowski, just made up the name, and Stanley was a Pittsburgh guy, doing these commentaries, dropping the references that only true Pittsburghers would know. Listeners knew I wasn't faking it. They said, "Hey, he's one of us, man." That started to grow the connection between me and my audience.

Dennis Miller gave me my first big comedy break. There was this little club in Oakland called Portfolio; it was Tuesday night and I was up last. Dennis grabs me and says, "I think you got some chops. Promise me you'll come back next week." We were fairly close, and I opened for Miller's act, a vote of confidence for any comic.

I didn't realize my stand-up act was honing my skills for radio. At the time, DVE was seventeenth in the market; they had just lost Jimmy and Steve, and they were rebuilding. Scott Paulsen was the morning host, and we hit it off. He was a brilliant radio personality, a brilliant writer and a really talented guy. We became Paulsen and Krenn and said, "Let's do *Saturday Night Live* on the radio." It led to a twenty-four-year career, and [I] discovered that this is a great town to have your face on a billboard.

JOY TAYLOR

Joy Allison Taylor is a media personality and television host for Fox Sports 1. She is currently the co-host of Speak *with LeSean McCoy and Emmanuel Acho. Taylor was the news update anchor on Fox Sports 1's* The Herd *with Colin Cowherd, and the host of* The Joy Taylor Show *Saturdays on Fox Sports Radio. Taylor previously served as the moderator for Fox Sports 1's studio show* Skip and Shannon: Undisputed *with commentators Skip Bayless and Shannon Sharpe.*

I love Pittsburgh. It is a place that is very down to earth and carries a certain kind of toughness about it. It's a place I will always have love for, being born and raised there. That's where I get my sports roots from.

If you've spent any time in Pittsburgh, then you know what sports means to the city of Pittsburgh. If you're from Pittsburgh, you're a sports fan. It's very much a part of the culture of the city and kind of the fabric that keeps Yinzers together. I was definitely a jock in high school. Some of my earliest memories are of football, being at the Wolf Arena in Turtle Creek. I remember when they tore down Three Rivers Stadium. Some of my core memories are just around sports. I played sports growing up, going to the basketball courts—I wanted to be Michael Jordan, which was not in the stars for me—and you're running track and soccer at Woodland Hills…sports was just such a big part of the community.

When I'm asked about how I got into sports, it's always kind of been a weird question to me because that's always been the norm for me. The Steelers—everyone I know is a Steelers fan. You care about the Steelers, and you're watching the game. And you have an opinion about the game or what's going on. So sports has just always been a part of my DNA. Being a woman who's passionate about sports has always been a part of my surroundings, and that was a part of my upbringing. It definitely was a big part of my childhood and some of my best memories.

If you're from Pittsburgh, you just understand what it is. It's something that doesn't really need to be said that you're just you're going to work hard, and you're going to take pride in what you do. There's just a sense of just being grounded that doesn't need to be spoken amongst people from Pittsburgh. I think throughout my

Courtesy FS1.

life, a lot of the experiences that I've had, I've been able to tap into that energy of being from Pittsburgh. It's like there is a humbleness and there are no shortcuts to being great. I think there's a lot of ties around the city with that, not taking shortcuts, really putting in the work and having a pride being where you are from, and I think that's something that a lot of people in Pittsburgh share.

I always wanted to be a personality. I loved listening to the radio growing up and hearing the way a really good host would make you feel like you're in the room with them. I think the traditional radio format helped establish a sense of community, especially locally, with media and fans. It becomes a part of your routine.

I also want to give the opportunity to younger broadcasters and women in the business who don't often get booked on national shows to come on and give their opinions as well. That's always important to me when I give opportunities to pay it back. You'll hear more women on my show than others, and that's intentional. I'm hoping that we are introducing some amazing women in the business to new audiences. That's important to me.

I'm in Los Angeles now, a far, far cry from my home in Turtle Creek that I grew up in. When I was a kid, I had a little neon news desk with the clothes hamper. We put a sheet over it and you had the hairbrush as a microphone, and you did the news. We would do that in my bedroom that I shared with my sister 'til I was sixteen. When I finally got on the show that I'm on now, which is my first full-time show hosting opinion, it's what I've been aspiring to my whole career.

It was really funny to sit back and think about that experience, just being a little girl in Pittsburgh in my bedroom with my sister and my neighbor, playing news anchor and to now being here in Los Angeles. It has been a really crazy, wild journey, a wild life, but I think it's really special to be from a place like Pittsburgh, where you always have grounded people reminding you of what hard work is, what being inspired really means, and that was that was a fundamental memory to call back to when that when that moment happened.

I'm looking forward to watching a really great Steelers season this year. I love the 'Burgh very much. I am a proud Yinzer. Shout out to Woody High and all my family and friends in Pittsburgh. Here we go Steelers!

LARRY RICHERT

Since September 2001, Larry Richert has hosted the KDKA *Radio Morning News, part of Audacy Pittsburgh. Richert has been a constant in Pittsburgh radio and television since the early '80s. He has long been an ambassador for the City of Pittsburgh and was winner of the Vector's Richard Caliguiri Award for that reason.*

I'm a Pittsburgh guy, grew up in Millvale…my mom was from Millvale, my dad from Woods Run on the north side, so when they got married they moved to where my mom was on the main drag in Millvale. And my mom's family and relatives, it's kind of a crazy, quintessential Pittsburgh thing where my aunts, uncles, were all within a very small footprint in Millvale. I never realized how tiny it was because we moved when my dad got a job in Wexford, and we moved out to Wexford when I was three, which was like the northwest territory. That was my backyard growing up, and I ended up going six years to Catholic grade school at St. Ursula. Most of the kids I went to grade school with went to Hampton High School, then I went to North Allegheny.

When I was a senior, North Allegheny had just built the new high school and they put in a color television studio, but they really didn't know what to do with this new technology. They created a pilot program for twelve students, and I was one of them and I really fell in love with TV and radio. Our first job was to put together a three- to five-minute video story together—almost a mini-news story—and we would work together as crew members on each other's projects.

Well, I narrated my own project. They showed it to the school board, and school board members said, "I thought this was for the students." The teacher said, "It is for the students." "Well, where did they get that narrator?" And she said, "That's one of my students." As important as any positive reinforcement is, that gave me a little confidence to say, "Maybe I can do this."

Since my dad worked so hard and wanted to get an education, he pushed education, self-discipline, find your passion. He would put motivational stickers on the mirror in the bathroom—positive attitude, enthusiasm, set your goals, self-discipline. My friends used to come and they'd make fun of it, but it stuck. My dad created a patch that said, "Master self-discipline and become a mental millionaire." So he said, "Don't worry about the money. Find your passion, do something you're passionate about and the money and success will come."

I graduated from high school, then stayed home a year to work because I needed to make some money so I could afford to go to school. So I worked at a foreign car dealership—it was a small place—and I was the parts guy. I used to drive an El Camino stick shift, and the radio only got AM so I listened to KDKA and WTAE with O'Brien and Garry; they were this duo back then that on April Fools' Day they played "Pineapple Princess" by Annette Funicello every song. I'm hearing this and I'm thinking, "That's what I want to do. I can do that, have fun like those guys do." Unbeknownst to me, my buddy goes to Clarion, and I was enrolled at Edinboro, two weeks before school starts, he goes, "Lar, I'm doing this radio thing at school. You gotta come here and do this." I switched schools, joined the radio station. I knew that I loved this, but I wondered if I could ever make a living doing this.

I still didn't think I could get a real job, but I got an opportunity at Y108, the country station, which is now part of the Audacy Group, and it was in the Fulton Building, downtown. I had a friend who was my program director in college—he was a senior when I was a freshman—he got a job at WEEP and WDSY, and he was the one who opened the door, got me to send a tape and got me an audition. A guy named Ted Sohier, who is still around at WQED Radio, gave me my first big shot in the commercial world in Pittsburgh.

It sounds glamorous to say "Oh, you got to the big time in Pittsburgh," but WDSY played popular country music like they did on elevators for Muzak where it was orchestrated. So they dubbed it the Daisy Country Orchestra, and the liners were "WDSY, fresh like a spring time breeze." I realized that for me to go up, I needed to go out, leave the city and come back. I got a call that day—day one—from radio station WRIK, and the program director was from Mount Washington. And he told me he was going to make me an offer I couldn't refuse. He says, "You can do afternoons, 3:00 p.m. to 6:00 p.m., five days a week." The music was contemporary music—the Spirit of the Palm Beaches—and the bonus was it was only a mile from my townhouse.

I was there about a year plus, and I was getting antsy so I sent out tapes. I missed home, was only getting paid $200 a week, so I sent tapes to Detroit, Boston and WTAE Radio in Pittsburgh. I got a call from Ted Atkins, legendary general manager, they were in the same building as the TV station, and they flew me up on People's Express, in the winter, snow flying sideways, and I thought do I really want to do this. I mean I'm living in West Palm Beach. I met with Ted, booming voice, came from Los Angeles, smoked cigarettes. The job turns out to be *Saturday Nights at the Oldies*, six big hours of playing records, then a Sunday afternoon shift and three days a week. I was a producer. So twenty-seven grand, which is more than I was making….I thought I died and went to heaven. At the end of that one-day visit, I learn there's a lot of production, or as Ted said, "It's a goddamn hornet's nest back there, but do you want the job or not?" Right on the spot, and I was afraid to say no. I said, "I'll take it Mr. Atkins." So I flew back to Florida, gave my notice, packed up and flew back home.

I worked there six years on the AM and FM, which at the time was WHDX, and worked with O'Brien and Garry and then with Jack Bogut when he came to WTAE. A couple of years later, I go to KDKA, work with John Cigna and get my own television show. When I was in high school, I worked at a Ponderosa Steak House, and the bun girl was Jocelyn Howell, who becomes executive producer at KDKA TV, and the late Lorraine Sneebold. Sue McInernny, the news director, got me an audition for *KD Country*. I figured that was my shot in TV. But I did a stand-up at the Funny Bone comedy club that my brother Patrick videotaped. Lorraine says, "Can I borrow this?" shows it to the KDKA TV general manager. It was New Year's Eve, and it became "How about him for our morning variety show?" A couple of years later, I became the weather man for TV….They sent me to AccuWeather and learn the computers and equipment, which I did for ten years.

But I was missing life working at night, with my kids. I was forty, so I prayed to land another job and stay in Pittsburgh. Luckily, the GM of KDKA Radio called and said, "John Cigna is going to retire, would you be interested?" I succeeded Cigna, who was the host of the morning show for eighteen years. We did the big reveal on a Harley in Gateway Center. Five days later, 9/11 happens, and the whole world changes and the focus of the station changes. More than twenty years later, I'm still here.

LYNNE HAYES-FREELAND

Lynne Hayes-Freeland got her start at KDKA-TV in the mid-1970s working as a production assistant and then as a field producer on Evening Magazine. *She created* Weekend Magazine *and produced* Vibrations, *a forerunner to* The Lynne Hayes-Freeland Show, *which she began hosting in the 1980s. She also produced the annual* Children's Hospital Free Care Fund Telethon *and moved into the news department as an on-air reporter in the late 1980s.*

I was fortunate to have grown up in Schenley Heights, a tight-knit predominantly African American neighborhood tucked between Oakland and the Hill District during the early 1960s. That neighborhood was idyllic, and a bond grew during a significant daily walk down a set of city steps into Oakland to the former Henry Clay Frick School.

It seemed that there were hundreds of these steps. I would never walk up these steps today. But that's what we did. We walked up and down those steps every day. Then in the winter, because there was grass next to the steps, that's where we would go sled riding when there was snow. That was some of the best sled riding around.

All the kids, we all walked together in a group so there were like twelve to fifteen of us. I was probably the youngest, but I got to walk with them because my older sister was in the group. There were some kids who lived a block or two beyond us. And they would come down and we would be at the corner of our street, and we'd go another block and there would be another group of kids. Those were fun times, when I think back on them, because we did everything together.

While Schenley Heights is a stone's throw from Oakland, our group

Courtesy Jordan Beckham/KDKA Radio.

didn't hang out there. We went straight to school, and we came straight home. The most we did is linger on the steps coming home, but we were not allowed to deviate from that route at all....If you deviated from that, you would have been by yourself. We all had to hold each other accountable.

With one rare exception, every now and then, we might sneak and go into Gus Miller's, the newsstand at the corner of Forbes and Atwood that was a neighborhood institution for decades.

I was kind of the wild child. My biggest break from my neighborhood happened when I went to St. Paul's Cathedral, now part of Oakland Catholic, for high school, unlike my classmates and sister, who attended the original Schenley High School. The principal at Frick called my mother in and said, "Lynne's a really bright girl, but she's easily distracted. She needs a little more discipline." Presented with the option of attending the all-girls school or Taylor Allderdice for high school, where my mom taught, I opted for the Catholic school and remain a proponent of single-sex education to this day.

It was the best thing that my parents could have done for me. At that point, there were not many African American students at St. Paul's. There were nine Black girls in my class. It gave me a different perspective and a different understanding of being a minority.

I graduated in 1973, left the neighborhood for college and to start a family, but returned to my family home—like many others—to take care of my aging parents. My father, who is ninety-seven, still lives with me. It's very much a part of African American culture to take care of aging family members. I'm not saying that doesn't happen in other communities, but it very much happens in the African American community.

I was actually a business and accounting major in college, but I didn't do so well in business. During my sophomore year, I started dating a guy studying journalism/broadcasting, and that's how I was introduced to the radio station. I knew that was my calling. I got a job in the business; he didn't.

I was on air for more than thirty-five years. Broadcast was always a focus—news reporting was not. It was just something that I landed in. Everyone always told me I should be on the radio because I've always had a deep voice. To be honest, I wanted to be a jazz DJ with a radio station. In fact, while at Duquesne University, I was the jazz show host for the student radio station.

After college, I spent my first fifteen years in broadcasting as a producer. I joined KDKA-TV in 1976 to produce the *Roy Fox Show* and later took on the *Evening Magazine* program. It wasn't until 1981 that I moved to the station's programming department to produce *Vibrations*, which was our weekend magazine programming at the time. When the host left to take a job at CBS Chicago, I was asked to host the show, which eventually became *The Lynne Hayes-Freeland Show* on KDKA-TV.

When Marty Griffin went on medical leave, Marty called me and asked if I could fill in for him on the radio. I was excited for the opportunity because as a reporter, I was tired of being outside in the cold, on the side of the road at midnight. This gave me the opportunity to do what I love to do.

People always ask me, "What's been the most important aspect of your career?" For me, it's not talking about the big stories I've covered or the big names of people I've interviewed. It's the stories that have changed people's lives. It's the woman who comes up to me and say, "Thank you. I got my mammogram because of what you said yesterday." It's the child that says, "Mrs. Freeland, I want you to meet my new mom." I know we've made a difference when we've changed lives. I'm making that an obligation to live up to.

As far as stories that I've reported on, interviewing Nelson Mandela one year after his release from prison was memorable, not only because of who he was but also because he ended up being such a different person from what I expected. He was quiet, soft-spoken, and before he sat down, he offered me a cup of coffee.

I recently started going through my records, and after seeing the list of names I've interviewed—Rosa Parks, James Baldwin, the list goes on—I immediately felt truly blessed. It still amazes me that I've had the honor to be in their presence.

RICK SEBAK

For going on forty years, Rick Sebak has been a charming, dimple-smiled presence as he's wandered about town, telling stories about all the things that make Pittsburgh worth calling home. His documentaries have been a fixture on WEQD-TV, including tasty half-hour travelogues, bites of history and musings about why we all love donuts and hot dogs.

Although I was born inside the Pittsburgh city limits at the old South Side Hospital in June 1953, my parents had already been living in a comfortable little yellow brick house on Sylvania Drive in Bethel Borough for four years. When my parents moved there, my mother's mother allegedly asked, "If you get pregnant, how will the doctor ever find you?" Bethel was still in the boonies to some city-dwellers like my grandmother, but it was actually a well-established community with a long history of farming and coal mining, and it was enjoying the postwar boom of families like ours relocating to the "burbs."

I soon found out that I had an older brother called Skip who had preceded me by eighteen months. He taught me basics from walking and talking to making the most of Christmas in our neighborhood.

Courtesy Visit Pittsburgh.

But I think anyone who grows up here has a certain amount of Pittsburgh pride. And I remember one summer, the summer after my first grade year, I got to go to the Falk School. It was for gifted and talented kids, or something like that, and my mom made a deal with them that she would drive me to Oakland from Bethel Park every day if they would take my older brother too. She said, "I'll drive Rick if you take Skip too." And so they agreed to that. And she literally made every day this great adventure. We would either go to the Carnegie Library or the museum, or we would have a picnic in Schenley Park. We would do something really cool. Or we'd go to Hazelwood to see the things that she used to do when she was a little girl. That was a really incredible summer, and those things all played a role in my initial love of Pittsburgh, which was then renewed when I moved back in '87.

I grew up in Bethel Park, then went to school at UNC in Chapel Hill, got my first job in South Carolina and worked there in public television for eleven years before I answered an ad in a trade journal and got my job at WQED. But the first job had all kinds of Pittsburgh connections. My mother sent me a *Pittsburgh Press* article by Barbara Holsopple; she would write these columns, and it included an item about Josie Carey doing a children's soap opera in South Carolina. It was 1971, and I happened to be looking for a summer job so I sent her a letter. Josie was a big star at WQED and KDKA when I was little, and she invited me to come to the station in Columbia, South Carolina, where she told me they would take me on as a summer intern.

It was a magical summer working on a show called *Wheee!* where Josie wrote the songs and the music was done by Joe Negri, so there were lots of Pittsburgh connections. But that was my start in television with Josie Carey...

she's my mentor, she gave me my first job in television and she helped start WQED in 1953.

I feel lucky and grateful that I've been able to make so many programs, both for WQED and PBS, and I think Pittsburgh was, is and probably will be for a long time a wonderful place to be, work and to goof around.

Right now, I think Pittsburgh's mix of new, hip culture and older, more traditional blue-collar, gritty, hardworking traditions, neighborhoods, restaurants and bars, along with our incredible history as an industrial workshop where giant fortunes were made, gives us a wonderful variety of options, sites for exploring and makes for captivating stories. The mix is the key I think.

Having been away from '71 to '87, I came back with some fresh eyes. That's when I came to the realization that there's a lot to like here. And what an interesting history we have. As the nineteenth century became the twentieth century, we were a world capital, one of the most important places on Earth. All this industry was happening here, and oil was discovered just one hundred miles north of Pittsburgh. I just loved all that stuff. You know, it's really weird that thirty-six years later, I still feel that excitement.

What I love about Pittsburgh is that it is endlessly fascinating and perpetually surprising. I still learn things all the time, like Pittsburgh has the highest percentage of native-born residents of any major American city. Part of that is Pittsburghers just love this place....There are the family connections, the depth of commitment, this crazy topography and why we have so many boomerang people.

I remember when I did my *Downtown Pittsburgh* show we went to the Arrott Building at 4th and Smithfield. We liked it because it looks like it has stripes. And it's a first-generation skyscraper, which means that it's between ten and fourteen stories tall because that's how far an elevator could take you at the time. I looked into the history of Arrott—the guy who built it—and he was the guy who figured out that you could put enamel on iron and make a bathtub. He did it here in Pittsburgh, and he called his company Standard Manufacturing. And it still exists as American Standard. You'll see it on toilets and urinals. He was the bathtub millionaire.

I still get this thrill out of learning this stuff. Because Pittsburgh's this interesting place where unexpected things happen, like bathtubs.

PATRICE KING BROWN

Since addressing Congress at the age of sixteen as runner-up to Miss Teenage America, Patrice King Brown's professional life has been a remarkable journey. A fixture on local television for more than thirty years, she began a broadcasting career at a Pittsburgh radio station and then was quickly hired at CBS affiliate KDKA-TV as a co-host for Pittsburgh 2Day, *a popular talk/variety show. Following her success on* Pittsburgh 2Day, *Brown became a KDKA news anchor at 4:00 p.m., 6:00 p.m. and 11:00 p.m. Through the years, Brown earned numerous awards for her work as a reporter, talk show host and news anchor, including being the recipient of the Board of Governor's Emmy award from the National Academy of Television Arts and Sciences—an Emmy for Lifetime Achievement in Broadcasting.*

I'm from a family that we always called those chatty King kids. I have an older brother and a younger brother, and we used to read all the time. I think that's what sparked our interest in storytelling and the ways stories are told. They never pushed us toward television or film—we just did it. Once that got our imagination going, we put on shows all the time at home. Instead of telling us to go sit down somewhere, our parents encouraged us. We were always that gabby group of kids. The music, the movies and TV always brought us together as a family. Our parents were the cool parents who listened to cool music and knew the words to the songs.

We were TV kids, most of us who grew up in the '60s were, and we would watch different shows. I remember thinking very early on—and as it turns out I wasn't alone in that thinking—I could do that. But I didn't realize that there might have been barriers to me doing that, racial barriers. As a kid you don't understand that, but as it turned out it was not to be at all.

When I was sixteen, I was in a pageant, which is something I don't talk about often, but I ended up being Miss Teenage Pittsburgh and a runner-up in the nationally televised Miss Teenage America. World Book was a major sponsor, and it was a scholarship pageant, not a beauty pageant. I had to take a three-hour exam, and that set me on a path of speaking engagements across the state about teenage issues during my junior year in high school. That started a fun and busy year, but it also started my public life.

I always thought I would be a teacher, a reading specialist or an English teacher. But my first job was in sales at WTAE Radio—my first big job where I could earn more than I owed. Very fortunately, though, I landed at KDKA TV, which was an amazing experience on so many levels. I grew

Courtesy KDKA Television.

up with Larry Richert, Jon Burnett, Ken Rice, Harold Hayes—my TV brothers—and we all grew up together on KDKA.

When I first went on the air, I was hosting a show called *Pittsburgh 2Day*. My first day, I broke out in hives. The first day I was on the air. I mean, head to toe hives, I was so nervous. It was actually kind of a scary experience that day. *Pittsburgh 2Day* was fabulous though. Guests came to the studio; it wasn't done by satellite. The first person I had on the air was Charlton Heston. I was so excited to interview him, and in my mind, I'm talking with Moses. He came in, shook hands and talked, which was great. He said, "Call me Chuck." We had some of the biggest stars of the day, some of the most controversial, the athletes, the rock stars who always had fifty thousand people with them. Then you had someone like Charlton Heston or Gregory Peck, who came in alone—they just showed up. It was a fabulous experience for twelve years.

That's what kept going through my mind. A little girl from Sheraden talking to…fill in the blank. Once I began to think of myself as a liaison between our Pittsburgh audience and these wonderful folks who had a message, and they were "folks," then everything was just smooth sailing.

After Westinghouse canceled its talk shows, I was moved into news. I started as a health reporter and did health reporting for a while. That was my on the street work. And then they put me on with Larry Richert, and we co-anchored a morning show where I did the news. I was eventually promoted to where I was the senior female, and I was doing 4:00 p.m., 6:00 p.m. and 11:00 p.m., then 6:00 p.m. and 11:00 p.m., and going out on special projects.

The best part was I got to do this in the city that I grew up in. That's what was so exciting to me. I'm at home. I knew the people, I am the people. Pittsburgh was comforting and wonderful to work in. I've always been very proud of Pittsburgh and Pittsburgh history and love to share it with people. It's not just the Steel City, but we can't seem to escape that image. Pittsburgh is very grounding; the people are kind and helpful.

Family and community in Pittsburgh is everything. I think about my parents, my grandparents, the hard work that they did, the strong women who I stand upon their shoulders. I miss Pittsburgh, and leaving there I miss the feeling of community. I still think of Pittsburgh as home. There is no question about that. It's the 'Burgh girl transplanted, and I'm still trying to find my total role here in California. In Pittsburgh, people want all of us to do well, all of us to achieve. No matter how successful people become in Pittsburgh, for the most part, they remember from whence they came.

There is also such a sense of neighborhood...somebody gets hurt, somebody is ill, somebody passes away, these people are there for you. When KDKA did the Hometown Advantage campaign, we realized that so many of us were from Pittsburgh, which was really rare in a TV market. I knew when I would report on something that happened in McKees Rocks or Braddock or Fox Chapel, I knew where it was, I knew what it looked like. You can picture things. When the US Airways airplane crashed, and many of those people were from Upper St. Clair, you knew those people, too, and you feel for them. I always thought of the stories as people's lives, and many times, somebody I knew.

Overall, as television was growing, I was proud to be in that first generation of women to be on the anchor desk and to be one of the few African American women to make the anchor desk on a prime news broadcast because when that happened, I was one of three in the country. I brought all of my life experiences to your questions, to your thoughts, to everything you do. So I came from the perspective of a woman, a Black woman, a mother, a wife, a daughter, a teacher and a Pittsburgher, so you have that perspective when you interview someone. It is so ingrained in me.

I loved being in Pittsburgh and having people calling my name all of the time. But there is also something nice about going into a store and not having people say, "Patrice you don't want that." I'm very proud of the city and its people. I am also grateful for the support and the strength that they gave me and the friendship and the love. I miss my friends at the station a great deal. I also miss doing stories about the people of Pittsburgh. This is my home.

SOURCES

George Benson

Asbury Park Press. October 24, 2014.
Beaver County Times. May 13, 2015.
CBS Pittsburgh. May 13, 2015.
New York Times. December 12, 2020.
Red Bull Music Academy. December 12, 2014.

Antoine Fuqua

Complex. October 13, 2016.
Irish Times. August 16, 2018.
Pittsburgh Post-Gazette. September 30, 2021.
Pittsburgh Tribune Review. October 14, 2016.
YouTube. March 20, 2013.

Billy Gardell

Columbus Dispatch. May 22, 2015.
KDKA TV. September 23, 2019.
Next Pittsburgh. January 23, 2015.
Pittsburgh Tribune Review. July 28, 2022.

Jeff Goldblum

NBC Today Show. July 7, 2022.
Pittsburgh Post-Gazette. July 4, 2004.
Wall Street Journal. November 20, 2018.
WTAE TV. May 23, 2018.

Rob Marshall

Carnegie Mellon University. A conversation with Rob Marshall, March 26, 2012.

Billy Porter

Pittsburgh Post-Gazette. September 1, 2015.

Tom Savini

Smoke and Mirrors: The Story of Tom Savini. 2015.

ABOUT THE AUTHOR

Most kids aren't hooked on TV news, but for Dick Roberts it was a childhood obsession. Growing up in Ligonier, Pennsylvania, his favorite TV shows were newscasts, and he could name just about every important newsmaker, anchor and reporter on the national networks and local stations in Pittsburgh and Johnstown. Over the years, this obsession with news media evolved into a passion for storytelling, corporate communications and public relations and their potential to help shape how people perceive the world. After graduation from Duquesne University in 1976, Roberts began his career as an entertainment promoter with Dick Clark Concerts. On the belief that a company's most important asset is its reputation, he became a trusted adviser and strategic communications professional with the J. Walter Thompson Company and later his namesake firm, Roberts Communications USA, on leading, admired companies like Mellon Bank, Giant Eagle, U.S. Steel, Coors Brewing, Coca-Cola, Sprint, GNC, Sears, PGA Tour, PGA of America, Eat'n Park Restaurants, Pittsburgh Mercy Health System, MediVet and Salton Kitchen Appliances. As an advocate for helping prepare the next generation of communications professionals, Roberts serves as an instructor of advertising, public relations and digital media in the Rowland School of Business at Point Park University. In his downtime, he enjoys musical theater and piano jazz (despite a near total lack of musical talent) and admiring a classic golf swing.